Training Your Chihuahua

Mira Leibstein

BARRON'S

Cover Credits

Shutterstock: front cover, back cover, inside front cover, inside back cover.

All inquiries should be addressed to:
Barron's Educational Series, Inc.
250 Wireless Boulevard
Hauppauge, NY 11788
www.barronseduc.com

ISBN: 978-0-7641-4686-2

Library of Congress Catalog Card No. 2011007734

Library of Congress Cataloging-in-Publication Data
Leibstein, Mira.
  Training your chihuahua / Mira Leibstein.
    p. cm.
Summary: "Because the typical Chihuahua is fiercely loyal to its master, this little dog doesn't always get along well with strangers or children. Prospective owners of Chihuahuas are generally advised to include socialization methods in the dog's training when it is very young. This book, a title in Barron's Training Your Dog series, presents breed-specific advice to dog owners. The emphasis is on dog-friendly methods for teaching skills and preventing or correcting bad habits. Virtually every aspect of canine training is covered, including house training, teaching obedience to verbal cues and hand signals, retrieving, walking the dog on a leash, and more. Instructive color photos appear on most pages"—Provided by publisher.
  Summary: "This book tells the reader how to train a chihuahua. The author and the publisher consider it important to point out that the advice given in the book is meant primarily for normally developed puppies from a good breeder--that is, dogs of excellent physical health and good character. Includes Brief history of the breed. Explains body language, Virtually every aspect of canine training is covered, including housebreaking, teaching obedience to verbal commands and hand signals, retrieving, walking the dog on a leash, and more. Instructive color photos appear on most pages"-- Provided by publisher.
  Includes bibliographical references and index.
  ISBN 978-0-7641-4686-2 (pbk.)
  1. Chihuahua (Dog breed)--Training. I. Title.
  SF429.C45L45 2011
  636.76--dc22   2011007734

Printed in China
9 8 7 6 5 4 3 2

Photo Credits

Dreamstime: pages 2, 4, 12, 25 (top), 25 (bottom), 28, 30, 32, 36, 38, 39, 48, 49, 57, 80, 98, 114, 131, 138, 145; iStock: pages 23, 24, 27, 42, 116; Joan Hustace Walker: pages 11, 33, 42, 44, 50, 52, 53, 55, 56, 58, 62, 82, 85, 87, 88, 89, 90, 92, 97 (top left), 97 (top right), 97 (bottom), 103 (top left), 103 (top right), 103 (bottom), 109 (top left), 109 (top right), 109 (bottom), 120, 123 (left), 123 (right), 124, 125, 127, 134, 142, 143; Premier Products: pages 45, 47; Shutterstock: pages viii–ix, x, 1, 3, 5, 6, 8, 10, 16, 18, 20, 21, 22, 31, 34, 37, 40, 43, 46, 54, 59, 60, 67, 70, 75, 77, 78, 94, 106, 112, 115, 117, 128, 133, 135, 136, 140, 146, 147.

About the Author

Mira Leibstein, B.S., CPDT-KA is a professional dog trainer and animal behavior consultant, working with dogs, cats, and horses. She offers private and group skills instruction, behavior evaluations and modification programs, and shelter behavior consulting in the New York area. She is a volunteer for Pet Safe Coalition, a professional member of the Association of Pet Dog Trainers, an approved presenter for the Dogs & Storks program, and a Canine Good Citizen evaluator. She teaches a variety of classes and workshops for pet owners and other trainers, including clicker skills, scent work, tricks for pets, beginning dog sports, and socialization programs, and has launched the "Transitions: Your Baby and Your Dog" workshop with colleague John Visconti at area hospitals.

Acknowledgments

This book would not be possible without the support of my family, especially my husband, who tolerated the long hours, incessant chatting about Chihuahuas, and the occasional grumpy attitude during this project. Many thanks also go to the colleagues that encouraged me to get my words on paper, and to the editing team at Barron's for making the manuscript come to life. Lastly, thank you to all the dogs that have taught me to be patient, pay attention, and to look for the good things.

Important Note

This book tells the reader how to train a chihuahua. The author and the publisher consider it important to point out that the advice given in the book is meant primarily for normally developed puppies from a good breeder—that is, dogs of excellent physical health and good character.

Anyone who adopts a fully grown dog should be aware that the animal has already formed its basic impressions of human beings. There are dogs that as a result of bad experiences with humans behave in an unnatural manner or may even bite. Only people who have experience with dogs should take in such an animal.

Even well-behaved and carefully supervised dogs sometimes do damage to someone else's property or cause accidents. It is, therefore, in the owner's interest to be adequately insured against such eventualities, and we strongly urge all dog owners to purchase a liability policy that covers their dog.

Contents

10

Five Top Skills to Teach Your Chihuahua 95

11

Five Skills for Great Manners 113

12

Five Fun Things to Teach Your Chihuahua 121

13 Five Red Flag Behaviors 129

14 Spotlight on Chihuahuas 141

Recommended Resources 146

Index 148

1 Brief History of an Ancient Breed

A Mysterious Origin

The origin of the Chihuahua is shrouded in mystery, with competing theories as to where the tiny breed originated. Both folklore and archeological findings show that the breed as we know it today probably originated in the Chihuahua State of Mexico.

Purists like to speculate that the Chihuahua is the direct descendent of the ancient native Mexican Techichi, described as a small-stature, long-legged dog, heavy boned and long coated, with a thin almost fawnlike body, and a humped back. The Techichi was known to be kept by the Toltecs as a pet as early as 1100 A.D., and may have been used for religious rites. Paleontologists have collected remains of such a dog from as early as the fifth century A.D. from the central and southern regions of Mexico, as well as South America.

In addition, archeologists have recovered clay sculptures of small dogs that resemble a Chihuahua made by the natives of Colima beginning approximately 2,000 years ago. These clay dogs, often found in burial shafts, were thought of as guides through the underworld for the human soul to reach heaven. These charming clay dogs were made in a variety of sizes and positions, but many were enjoined pairs, referred to as the dancing dogs of Colima by archeologists.

Others have speculated that the Chihuahua was of European origin, perhaps brought to the New World by the Spanish from the island of Malta. A small dog existed on the island that possessed a natural molera, an extremely rare soft spot similar to a fontanel in human babies, on the top of the skull; the molera is also found in the Chihuahua. European paintings of the time, including Juan Bautista Martinez del Mazo's *Maria Teresa* (1638–1683), *Infanta of Spain*, include small dogs that closely resemble the Chihuahua. It would have been feasible for the Spanish to have brought along a popular pet that intermingled with the native dogs in Mexico, leading to the popular Chihuahua of today.

An alternate theory suggests that the Chihuahua was brought to Mexico by Chinese merchants during the 1700s. At that time, the Chinese were already recognized for dwarfing plants and animals, and it's possible they applied their talent to miniaturizing a popular pet of the time, perhaps crossbreeding their miniaturized pets with the endemic Techichi.

Whatever their origin, the tiny dog became a popular pet native to the area known as Chihuahua, bordering the Texas, Arizona, and New Mexico states. With the tiny breed's rise in popularity during the last century, Americans—and later Europeans—fell in love with what would become the modern Chihuahua.

The Modern Chihuahua

By the late 1800s the Chihuahua was on the scene in the United States as a companion animal and show dog. American dog lovers fell in love with the charming, personality-packed canine.

The first recorded entry of a Chihuahua in the United States was in 1884 at the Philadelphia Kennel Club show. The American Kennel Club exhibited Chihuahuas for the first time in 1890, in the "listed" dog class, a category designated for unregistered dogs.

The first Chihuahua was subsequently registered in the United States in 1903, and the breed was included in the American Kennel Club's (AKC) Toy Group by 1904. A Chihuahua champion was listed in the AKC's Stud Book by 1908.

The Chihuahua Club of America was established by 1923, along with a breed standard that largely remains unchanged today. During the early 1950s, fanciers revised the breed standard to include two varieties based on coat length: smooth-coated and long-coated.

Starting with that first group of fifty entries in the 1923 Chihuahua Club of American Specialty, the Chihuahua has exploded in popularity to be consistently ranked among the top ten breeds, with over 43,000 dogs registered by the early 2000s.

Along with this explosion in popularity in the United States comes the associated fame. Chihuahuas are seen everywhere in popular culture, from the hackneyed "Taco Bell" Chihuahua pushing tacos in the 90s, to the starring role in the 2008 Hollywood blockbuster *Beverly Hills Chihuahua*, which was a commercial hit and has grossed over $145 million worldwide to date.

Of course, the personality factor seems to increase as the breed gets smaller, so those pint-size cuties really pack a punch, especially when dubbed with witty dialogue and ad copy, making them ideal as the "breed of the month" for mass media and pop culture.

However, with such popularity comes a drawback: the overbreeding and disposal of millions of unwanted Chihuahuas. Experts say pop culture is to blame, with fans emulating Chihuahua-toting celebrities like Madonna, Paris Hilton, George Lopez, and Paula Abdul just to name a few, then abandoning the dogs when they realize this four-legged fashion accessory has needs for which they are responsible.

California shelters are inundated with abandoned Chihuahuas, with upward of 30 percent of the shelter population made up of the pint-size pups. One solution has been to ship the tiny dogs out of state to other shelters that have a small-dog demand that can't be met by their own supply, such as in the Midwest and Eastern states. Of course, that just spreads the love, so to speak, and doesn't really address the root of the problem: irresponsible breeding by people looking to make a quick buck selling puppies.

So as Chihuahuas reach market saturation and become the highly visible pets of the rich and powerful, you must take personal responsibility and make sure that the Chihuahua you bring into your life receives the same love, care, and attention that any other new addition to your family should have, because it's a loyal, intelligent, adorable dog and not merely a stuffed animal.

Packed with Personality

"A small dog with a big personality" is a common description of the lively Chihuahua. The breed is described by the official written standard by the Chihuahua Club of America as "graceful, alert, swift-moving, compact, and with a saucy expression." What's not to love?

There are some not-so-flattering descriptions, too, however. Most of the derogatory terms reflect the tendency for people to skip out on the socialization and training aspects of raising a small dog, leading to reactive, fearful, or aggressive responses when the dog is threatened or challenged.

While each pup certainly has an innate personality, inherited from mom and dad, we as pet owners do much to shape the pup's personality for better or worse, depending on the socialization experiences we expose the young pup to. However, "socialization" does not mean a wine and cheese party; it means exposing a puppy to a variety of people, places, and things with which he should be familiar and comfortable in adulthood, without scaring the daylights out of the little guy.

If the socialization experience is poor, or nonexistent, the pup will have difficulty adjusting to new situations and people as he gets older. And at only six pounds, if someone or something scares a Chihuahua they use the only defense at their disposal: They bite.

You will find that if your new pup is happy and confident, you can keep him that way with a good socialization plan. If your pup is shy or fearful, however, try to

double your efforts at gentle socialization, and get the help of a professional trainer or behaviorist while the pup is still young. Soon you will see your Chihuahua develop into the saucy, charming, and loving pet he should be.

Your Chihuahua: A Dog for Every Occasion

The Chihuahua as we know it today is the bouncy, personality-packed, popular pet that is at home in the pet household, a show home, doing therapy work, or on the agility course. He is ideal as company for the elderly or as a best friend for a gentle, responsible child. The Chihuahua is a popular choice for dog lovers from all walks of life.

Your Chihuahua can do everything a "big dog" can do, with a style all his own. Just because this is a small breed does not mean a Chihuahua is not clever or athletic. He can participate on the show circuit— and win! He can participate in dog sports such as scent work, obedience, Rally, and agility. Chihuahuas excel as trick dogs and always enjoy a walk in the great outdoors.

Whatever your interests or goals for your new pet, from faithful family companion to sports star, a Chihuahua could be the perfect choice for you.

2 *Chihuahua Behavior 101*

What's That Dog Saying? Reading Basic Body Language

It's not unusual for humans and dogs to "read" each other's intentions. Sometimes it seems that my dog knows things without any explanation whatsoever. However, it's more common that dogs and humans miscommunicate—sometimes with dramatic or even tragic results.

Miscommunication is so common that often dog behavior consultants can feel like translators going into people's homes for behavior consultations. Imagine the relief when dog owners learn what their dog is really trying to say with his body language. The dog often ends up glued to the "translator's" leg for the length of the session since he or she is the only person that speaks "dog" in the room. Both dog and human rely on the behavor consultants to break down the barrier of miscommunication.

So what's the magic of deciphering your best friend's language? A basic understanding of canine body language will get you far—after all, Chihuahuas don't speak English! Although the subtleties and finesse of dog communication are vast, a few strategies and some broad interpretations of your dog's behavior can help you communicate with your Chihuahua, and more importantly, can help your Chihuahua communicate with you!

A Wolf in Chihuahua's Clothing?

Going back approximately 130,000 years will get you started on understanding your little dog. A Chihuahua is a wolf in dog's clothing, sort of. Both dogs and wolves, in fact all of the canine species including foxes, coyotes, African wild dogs, and jackals, evolved from a common set of ancestors.

The history of dogs and their relationship with humans has undergone some rethinking recently, thanks to molecular dating methods that can determine evolutionary relationships. Recent DNA analysis suggests a date of about 130,000 years ago for the transformation of dogs from their wild ancestors. Some researchers consider modern dogs, *Canis familiaris*, a subspecies of the gray wolf, *Canis lupus*.

It's likely that as humans evolved, and subsequently settled in camps or villages that produced waste, the ancestor of the dog filled a niche. The dumps were an

Predation is a sequence of behaviors in succession, and functions in the capture, killing, and eating of prey. The basic canine predatory sequence is: orient (search), eye (alert to), stalk, chase, grab/bite, kill/bite, dissect, consume.

Although all species of canines have the same sequence of predatory behaviors, domestic dogs don't always retain the complete set, and some may skip sections altogether. For example, many hunting breeds have the first part of the sequence intact, but stop short of killing or eating what they retrieve. Some of the companion-type breeds, such as Chihuahuas, may have very little of the predatory sequence intact at all, which makes them ideal as house pets. Those dogs that are manic ball retrievers are repeating the *orient-eye-stalk-chase-grab* sequence, over and over again.

Often, your pet dog's predatory behaviors can be observed in play with objects such as balls or stuffed toys, which trigger the predatory sequence. Wave around a ball or that stuffed squirrel, and then throw it, watching your Chihuahua's reaction. Your Chihuahua may not chase toys at all, or he may chase them, bite them, and dissect them. Occasionally, the dog may consume the whole toy. Watching a dog play with a toy is like watching a predatory carnivore in action.

easy food source for those animals brave enough to use it. On occasion, the dogs were probably an easy food source for the people making all that garbage. Additionally, their alarm barking was a service the humans in the settlements may have found a liking for, so they didn't chase the scavengers off the premises.

Sometimes looking at the language of other canine species can shed some light on the language of modern dogs. Animal behavior researchers, called ethologists, agree that domestic dogs act very much like wolves, or more accurately wolf pups, in some contexts. However, it's not across all contexts, and certainly dogs have been domesticated long enough to form their own behavioral repertoire, sometimes quite different from their wild cousins.

A common example of how domestic dog behaviors can differ from wolf behaviors is the predatory motor pattern.

Chihuahua Communication

You can assume that your Chihuahua's behavior has some sort of intention, as crazy as that might seem sometimes.

Body Language Quick Reference

The table below shows some broad generalizations of dog body language.

	Neutral/Relaxed	Fearful/Stressed	Aggressive
Head	Normal carriage for breed	Low, ducking	High
Muzzle	Relaxed, no wrinkles on bridge of nose (unless normal for breed)		Wrinkled across bridge
Mouth	Relaxed lips, may pant or appear "smiley"	Mouth closed or tense lips drawn back at corners with panting/drooling, may be flicking tongue	Mouth closed, or tense lips retracted off teeth, or cheeks puffed
Whiskers	Relaxed along face	May be retracted flat to head, tense	Forward and tense
Eyes/ Eyebrows	Soft gaze, may be slightly closed, eyebrows moving	Whites showing, wild-eyed, panicky	Intense hard stare, often with obvious eyebrows and ridged forehead
Ears	Relaxed into normal carriage, moving	Back against side of head	Forward, tense
Hair Coat	Smooth	Hair may be falling out in clumps, often dandruff on dog	Fur raised along back, fluffed up all over body, or raised along tail
Body	Soft, relaxed	Crouched, cowering, tense	Erect, weight forward, stiff-legged and tense
Tail	Relaxed tail, held at back level, or tail wagging side to side or propeller style	Low carriage, stiff, held under belly, may be wagging slightly	Slow, stiff wag with tip only, or with tail straight up or over back

Social behavior or signals that are directed at people or other dogs, with intention, is communication. Chihuahuas routinely communicate to their two-legged family members using a range of signals, including playful, fearful, and aggressive communication.

How fluent is the average dog owner at reading dog body language? Can you read the signals of your Chihuahua and know what he is saying? Not always, since the signals are subtle (sometimes happening in the blink of an eye), usually happening in clusters with other behaviors that affect the meaning, and may vary according to context. For example, even a tail wag from your Chihuahua can convey different meanings, including arousal (sometimes happy, sometimes threatening), excitability, affiliation or friendliness, anxiousness, or aggressive threat. The meaning of the tail wag may vary depending on the other behaviors seen in the cluster, such as ear position, hackles, lip and eye positions, body weight distribution, and the height of tail carriage.

What areas of canine communication should you become familiar with to understand your Chihuahua? The broad behavioral categories, and the communication signals that occur with them, that will affect your ability to understand your Chihuahua include play behaviors, fearful behaviors, and aggressive behaviors. Let's go through them to learn a few basics. First review the Body Language Quick Reference to become familiar with typical body language your Chihuahua may exhibit when feeling relaxed and happy, fearful or aggressive. Keep in mind that a dog may show combinations of more than one emotional state (for example his fur is up along the back and he is crouched or, with a tense body and drooling) and can move back and forth between fear and aggression very quickly, depending on how threatened he feels. It's wise to evaluate the situation closely if your Chihuahua's body language moves out of the neutral range for any reason.

Play Signals

Play communication is one of the easiest things to recognize in a Chihuahua. Many play signals that dogs give each other are also given to other species, including humans. So what are the most commonly seen play signals?

People seem to recognize the face of a playful dog. Most people respond to a dogs "play face" (yes, that is a scientific term), by smiling back at the dog—it's easily read across species. The play face dogs give each other, and us, is characterized as slightly panty, with the lips retracted, loose jawed, ears pulled back, and it looks like the dog is smiling. The rest of the dog is relaxed and tail is wagging with the big, side to side, hip level wag that characterizes friendliness, or even in big circles, propeller style.

Occasionally, someone not very experienced with dogs is taken aback by the play face because the dog's teeth are showing, and they're under the impression that if a dogs teeth are visible, he must be aggressing. See how easy it can be to make mistakes about dog communication by paying attention to just one signal?

Another commonly seen signal, between dogs and from dogs to people is the "play bow." This exaggerated posture can be described as "butt in air, elbows on the floor," often with the above-described play face and wagging tail. Your Chihuahua in this stance is ready for a game, so join in!

One of the common concerns about play is that sometimes it looks like aggression. Remember, play is essentially the practice of adult behaviors such as predation, reproduction, and social relations, so when dogs play they use the body language that would be seen in those contexts. Often, the ways that we commonly play with our dogs rely on stimulating that predatory sequence we talked about earlier: owner jazzes dog up with toy, owner tosses toy, dog chases and retrieves toy, all

based on the predation sequence. Even just giving the dog a chew toy is a way to stimulate the other end of the sequence: grab, bite, dissect, consume.

Sometimes, play can spill over into outright aggression. Predatory drift can occur in social situations when one dog triggers a predatory response in the second, usually much larger, dog. This can be triggered by the smaller dog if it yelps, panics, or struggles during a scuffle in a manner to trigger the predatory motor pattern described previously. Social interactions between Chihuahuas and larger dogs, or predatory breeds, should be monitored carefully, and interrupted if the intensity gets overheated. Even a gentle larger dog can inadvertently injure a tiny dog, triggering a tragic chain of events resulting in death or injury of a small dog. Better to encourage size matched playmates on a regular basis as an outlet for all that playful energy!

What makes social play different from fighting are the clusters of calming signals and pausing that indicate that the play is not turning into something else. These clusters of context-specific signals indicate that "we're still playing!" Remember, dogs don't have hands, so they play with their teeth.

Often puppies will get into heated mock battles, wrestling and chasing each other. As the arousal level increases, play is frequently broken off while the dogs pause, sometimes sniff or engage in another activity for a few seconds, and then play resumes, often with the dogs switching roles from prey to predator and

> **Calming Signals**: *Calming signals, a phrase coined by acclaimed dog trainer Turid Rugaas[1], are hypothesized to be indicators that a dog is stressed and wants to resolve potential conflict, often by increasing the distance between individuals. Ethologists sometimes refer to these behaviors as "distance increasing behaviors" or "stop signals."*
>
> [1]*On Talking Terms With Dogs- Calming Signals, 2nd Edition, Turid Rugaas, 2006*

back again. Even when the dogs practice the repertoire of potentially aggressive behaviors, such as stalking, chasing, pouncing, growling, biting, and head shaking, there is a lack of intensity in the postures, and the dogs remain relaxed, with frequent pausing and other signals such as a lack of direct eye contact to indicate that it's all in good fun.

Fear Signals

So, why is it important to recognize fearful behavior in your Chihuahua? After all, if your Chihuahua isn't the bravest dog on the block, you're there to protect him, right? Unfortunately, not all Chihuahuas love the limelight, and many genuinely prefer the company of a few gentle companions, not a busy, boisterous lifestyle.

A fearful, timid, or shy Chihuahua is unhappy in situations that stress him. Fearful body language, such as shaking,

Calming Signals

Signal	Looks like	Possible meanings
Head turns	Can be a subtle, brief shift of head in one direction, or dramatic turn of head and held for several seconds. Functionally diverts the gaze.	I'm not a threat, you are approaching me too fast, or you are in my space, please slow down.
Turning away	Turning the side or back to another individual, may also sit or lay down	Calm down!
Soft eye	Softening of the gaze, may look like eyes are slits or closed	I'm calm, not a threat, and non-confrontational. I'm looking at you but not making hard eye contact.
Tongue flicks	A quick flick of the tongue over the nose	I'm a little nervous, please calm down.
Freezing	Stopping movement momentarily, often with head turn	I am not a threat.
Yawning	Occurs during high-tension situations, dog may also exhibit tense panting	I am stressed, uncertain, or nervous.
Sniffing	Sudden sniffing during social situations with other dogs or humans.	Functions to slow down or pause during play.

cowering, or frantic panting can be a big clue that your Chihuahua is not emotionally comfortable. You can help him overcome that fear and increase his quality of life, especially if your Chihuahua is young.

Generally, Chihuahuas will be fearful of new people, places or things if they have not been exposed to them during the developmental stages of puppyhood, a process called socialization. Socialization is critical for healthy adulthood, and is difficult at best after five or six months of age. So, a fearful adolescent or adult Chihuahua is often an indicator that the puppy was not well-socialized, or was frightened during the socialization process.

Good socialization not only teaches a puppy that specific things are not to be feared, it also has a cumulative effect—in general the more frequently a puppy is exposed to novel things the less fearful he will be as an adult to novel things.

If your Chihuahua is exhibiting fearful body language, typically crouching with ears back, tail tucked, and displaying calming signals, take note. Your Chihuahua is telling you that something or someone is threatening him, and to give him more room. Try gentle reintroduction later, and take care not to force exposure - that will only make the fear worse!

Aggression

There is a wide array of aggressive behaviors that any dog has the potential to exhibit. Ethologists identify over a dozen different kinds of aggression, ranging from maternal aggression, the hormonally mediated defense of offspring, to food-related aggression, a subset of resource guarding. Defining the term itself is complex and controversial, and its definition is still hotly debated by ethologists.

For our discussion here, aggression can be described as the threat of harmful behavior directed toward another dog or human to resolve conflicts due to threat or challenge. Many aggressive threats are ritualized social behaviors used to communicate information in order to avoid combat, since actual fighting is not a good long-term strategy for survival of the species.

Although aggression is one of the most commonly diagnosed behavioral problems seen in dogs, it can be difficult to effectively modify. Effective modification

requires experience in identifying what kind of aggression the dog is displaying, determining how long the behavior has been occurring, setting up good management and designing modification plans to change the behavior.

The more common types of aggression that the average Chihuahua owner will be exposed to include fear or stranger aggression (when threatened by people or strange dogs), territorial aggression (when people enter an environment the dog considers defendable, including houses, cars, and yards), and resource guarding (when retaining resources including food, toys, his people, or places such as beds, couches, or chairs).

Chihuahuas have a reputation that precedes them when it comes to aggressive tendencies. But its fierceness does not mean that a Chihuahua is a bad or mean dog. Aggression is not a moral statement made by the dog; it is a behavioral response to a social situation. Your Chihuahua is for some reason threatened in that context and is trying to put a little distance between him and the perceived threat by showing those teeth, or perhaps he feels a resource is threatened and will fight to retain ownership of it.

So, what do you need to know? If your Chihuahua is threatening a person or another dog, take note of the situation. If it happens on a regular basis or is predictable, it's time to get the help of a professional positive-reinforcement trainer or behavior consultant. Do not try to follow the advice of well-meaning, but often off-base friends that are "sure" of how to fix things. It's likely you will end up threatening your Chihuahua more and making it worse. Chihuahuas are tiny, but a bite still really hurts!

The D Word! Is My Chihuahua in Charge?

One of the commonly held myths for the last quarter century, and without a doubt the most detrimental for pet dogs, is that dogs displaying a variety of challenging, threatening, or aggressive behaviors are dominant.

Dominance has been attributed to just about every behavioral problem, including biting, house soiling, resource guarding, leash pulling, and food snatching, among others. Recommendations range from rank-reduction programs to physical intimidation and punishing, abusive handling such as hanging, scruff shaking, and alpha rolling. Sadly, pet owners have been led to believe that their pet's life goal was to increase their status, and if they didn't maintain dominance over their dog, he would take over the reins and run the show. But dominance theorists are barking up the wrong tree.

Where did dominance theory originate? Early studies of captive wolves gave a somewhat skewed picture of wolves as aggressors vying for alpha status or higher rank, using threats of violence to keep others in line. Scientists described elaborate displays of aggression over resources that seemed to culminate in a consistent winner, the alpha, and the loser, some other low-ranking beast. Of course, people extrapolated this theory to apply to dogs, since they are just watered-down wolves, right?

Unfortunately, something was lost in translation. Those original researchers went on to look at packs of wild wolves. What they found turned their previous findings upside down. The wild packs were pairs of breeding wolves raising their offspring, both puppies and adolescents: a family unit. Adults took turns establishing rules and doling out resources to youngsters, and status was contextual and fluid. As youngsters came of breeding age, they left to start packs of their own. There were no outside interlopers trying to take over, challenging for status or fighting for resources. Those researchers went on to redefine their use of status-related terms such as "alpha," and now simply called them "breeders" or "breeding pairs."

In fact, further research by Raymond and Lorna Coppinger[1] has shown that modern dogs may not form a pack at all. They do not mate with the same individuals over time, or form stable alliances, like wolves or some other canines. Instead, they mate when the opportunity arrises, and go on their way, and the adult males do not provide resources for the resulting offspring or take part in raising them.

Dogs have a social structure that is opportunistic—if it's rewarding, and they can do it, they do it. If there is no pack, there is no point in fighting for status. Therefore, there is no need to resort to a flawed model based on mimicking aversive methods in order to enjoy the company of domestic dogs.

[1]Raymond and Lorna Coppinger, *Dogs: A New Understanding of Canine Origin, Behavior and Evolution,* 2001.

3 *Puppy Socialization*

Understanding Puppy Developmental Periods

Your Chihuahua goes from birth to adulthood at an accelerated pace. While humans have a leisurely eighteen to twenty years to acclimate to life on earth before they are responsible for making decisions for themselves, puppies have to habituate to, or become familiar and comfortable with, a variety of people, places, things, and other dogs before approximately sixteen weeks of age, when a hardwired increase in social fear interrupts environmental and social exploration.

If your puppy comes home at eight weeks, you only have eight more weeks to expose the little chap to other people, strange dogs, the experience of riding in automobiles, fireworks and other things that go boom, trips to the veterinarian and groomer, cats, babies in strollers, kids on bikes, delivery drivers, and so on. The list is endless, and there are only so many hours in a day. No wonder it's a challenge for most Chihuahua owners to get it right!

Becoming familiar with the major milestones of your puppy's development is the secret to successful socialization. The experiences your puppy has, and when he

has them, leave a lasting and profound impression that your puppy carries with him for the rest of his life.

A tremendous amount of socialization has already occurred by the time you get your Chihuahua puppy. In fact, the first two developmental periods have already flown by, and your puppy is almost done with the third developmental period if you bring him home at eight weeks of age.

The first developmental stage, the neonatal period, starts immediately at birth and lasts approximately two weeks. If you're very lucky, you will get to meet your potential puppy during this stage; be sure to take many photos, it goes fast! During the neonatal period the puppy's eyes and ears are closed, he has a limited sense of smell, and the primary motor skills seen are those needed for feeding, including sucking, swinging the head from side to side, and a slow forward crawl.

As the eyes open at around thirteen days old, the puppy moves into the second developmental stage, the transition period. This brief window, often no more than a week in duration, marks a fundamental change in nutrition, as the puppies still nurse but also begin to eat the semi-liquid, supplemental, partially digested food the mother provides. The first teeth erupt, and puppies are mobile enough to leave the nest to eliminate on their own. By the end of the transition period you see rudimentary social behavior between puppies, including play.

The third developmental stage is the social developmental period, lasting from three to twelve weeks of age. Many of the adult patterns of behavior are taking form, including social investigation, playful fighting, and sexual behavior. We see the first appearance of a critical fear period at approximately nine weeks. This fear period makes the pup particularly sensitive to environmental dangers into the tenth week, slowing down the rate of socialization temporarily.

Most people bring their new puppy home sometime near this initial fear period, so beware overwhelming a pup at this age with potentially startling experiences that may leave a lasting effect. A number of phobic reactions in adult dogs have their origins in experiences during this thankfully brief period.

The developmental stage most familiar to new puppy owners is the juvenile period. This is the stage from the social developmental period to sexual maturity, commonly referred to as adolescence. This period catapults the puppy to physical adulthood in a matter of months. Sometimes it seems the puppy physically and socially matures overnight, going from goofy, awkward, and playful with the attention span of a gnat, to athletic, focused, and more adultlike in their interactions with others.

Your Window of Opportunity

Why do all these developmental stages have such importance in the raising of puppies to be fit members of society? Because the experiences your Chihuahua has at each stage will affect his lifelong perceptions. For example, if your puppy's experience by sixteen weeks with strange children has been fun and yummy, he will probably like children later in life. If his experience is traumatic, or missing entirely, he may be suspicious and timid of children for the rest of his lifetime.

Of course, an adolescent or adult Chihuahua is capable of learning from new experiences. Many dogs are resocialized successfully after adoption as adults, but it is often difficult and slow. Before the age of sixteen weeks a puppy is more adaptable or receptive to new impressions. After sixteen weeks it becomes progressively more difficult for dogs to adapt. Poorly socialized, or undersocialized, puppies rarely reach their full potential as adults and are at risk for a variety of behavioral problems.

What Do Genetics and Early Experiences Have to Do with Behavior?

Nature versus nurture is an age-old debate in scientific literature. Modern scientists now know it's the combination and interplay of nature, or genetic predisposition, and nurture, the learning and socialization that occur after birth, that make up your adult Chihuahua's temperament.

Sometimes, behavioral characteristics can be attributed to the genetic predisposition of that dog. For example, a Golden Retriever puppy may be more inclined to pick up and return objects than your Chihuahua puppy. It's not that your Chihuahua cannot retrieve; it's simply that he must rely more on the nurture, or learning, of the skill rather than the genetic predisposition to just pick everything up.

Genetic predisposition to behavioral traits may also affect the socialization periods of your puppy. For example, fear periods are normal developmental stages that all puppies are subject to. It's possible that if mom had an early onset of social fear, say at eight weeks rather than the usual nine weeks, she can potentially pass this tidbit of genetic information onto her offspring. Presto! A genetic predisposition to early, and maybe stronger, fear imprinting in the next generation. So you can see that not only do the learned experiences your puppy has during the socialization period have importance on forming your adult Chihuahua's temperament but so does the genetic history of the generations before.

Potential puppy shoppers often hear the advice that they should meet the parents of their future pup. This is because the temperament of the parents of the pup is the best predictor of the temperament of the resulting offspring. If there is a behavioral red flag in one of those parents, such as profound shyness or unexplained aggression, you should not attribute it to poor socialization, as it may very well have a genetic component.

19

Introducing Your Puppy to People, Places, and Things

New puppy-raising owners should always make a plan for socialization. Though the initial experiences should be before sixteen weeks, plan to keep up the socialization game for the first two years of your puppy's life. You may miss a few things on the first pass, but the more often your pup experiences new objects or events, referred to as stimuli in behavior literature, the more likely he will be tolerant of new stimuli in the future.

Your primary goal with your new puppy should be to set up regular opportunities to expose your puppy to novel stimuli and help him get comfortable with them. Practice makes perfect, but it's good to set up a methodical approach that's similar each time. A typical socialization sequence includes first identifying a novel stimulus to approach or experience. Then, starting at a distance, begin a gradual approach toward the stimulus, watching the puppy for anxious body language, all the while using treats to make a good association with the presence of the stimulus. Don't be shy, it's impossible to make too good of an association with treats. In this case, more really is better!

Allow the puppy to investigate the new stimulus, as long as he is comfortable and relaxed. Whenever possible, encourage the puppy to interact with the stimulus, but if he is more comfortable at a distance that's fine too. People can feed the puppy treats, or he can eat treats off of or next to the new object, such as a bike or skateboard, or in the presence of running machinery or vehicles. When your puppy is done checking things out and seems happy and relaxed in the presence of this new stimulus, move on to the next experience.

There is a quick and relatively easy method to begin every puppy's socialization program with. It's an immersion program that exposes the puppy to a number of new stimuli over a period of months, including new places, a variety of people and dogs, and as many other experiences as possible.

For the first twelve weeks that your new puppy is home place his dinner, mixed with a few high-value goodies like chopped chicken, liverwurst, or hotdogs, in a Ziplock bag. Get in the car and head out to a different location. Perhaps stand in front of schools, supermarkets, train stations, gas stations, or walk in quiet residential streets, hang out in parking lots, parks, at street fairs, in the horse barn or dog park while the puppy eats his dinner one kibble at a time. If the puppy has not yet finished his immunization series, it is best to hold the young pup in your arms.

Have strangers of all types feed your puppy his dinner and pet him in exchange for whatever behaviors the puppy knows—sit, down, targeting, and tricks are a few examples. Be careful not to overwhelm the puppy; let the pup approach strangers at his own pace. Women get to give one kibble for each behavior, men give several, and children give several kibbles and a chicken chunk, hot dog slice, or other high-value yummy. In short, anything and anyone new should result in a yummy, and the more unusual the person, place, or thing, the better the yummy! If anything seems startling or overwhelming to the puppy, back away until the pup is relaxed again. When dinner is done, head home.

This gentle introduction to novelty makes huge strides in forming the stable adult temperament desired in Chihuahuas. Your dog at this point will have seen it all, and each new thing introduced will be no big deal. Very quickly, you and your puppy become experts in appropriate meet-and-greet behavior and adept at navigating new places and seeing new people and sites around town. After the initial twelve weeks of the program, gradually decrease the frequency

of, but never stop, these street sessions until by the end of the dog's second year you are going out once or twice a week to maintain the socialization set in place.

For pups that are unable to participate in these socialization sessions, due to illness, delayed immunization schedule, or any other reasons, bring the socialization home. Inviting friends and neighbors into your home several times a week and having them feed your puppy his dinner and play with him will make a tremendous difference in the socialization progress. Just remember to double your efforts when you have veterinary clearance to proceed. It is important to expose the pup to different locations and strange people. You can also bring the puppy into other people's homes with your veterinarian's approval, as long as any dogs present are otherwise healthy, well socialized, and immunized.

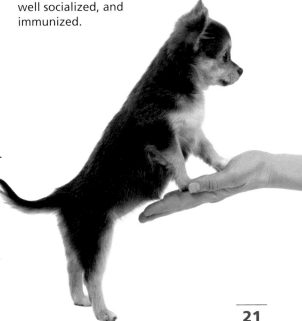

Making Good Associations with Classical Conditioning

Many of your new puppy's perceptions during the socialization period are made by predictive association, a phenomena called classical conditioning. This sort of conditioning is happening in the environment all the time, without us even trying. The regular appearance of a previously neutral stimulus predicts the appearance of a highly valued stimulus. Leashes are quickly associated with walks, doorbells are associated with strangers entering the home, the veterinarian in a white coat is associated with vaccinations (ouch).

You can use classical conditioning to help establish good associations, rather than just let bad associations happen.

For example, make trips to the veterinarian mostly predict fantastic food and games, rather than just an exam and needles. Make car keys and crating your puppy predict treat time, rather than alone time. Make the approach of strange, looming men on the street predict that the yummy piece of chicken comes out of your pocket. Good use of classical conditioning will help establish great associations, and weaken or even prevent other potentially bad associations.

What If My Puppy Is Scared?

It's not uncommon for a new stimulus to initially intimidate a Chihuahua puppy. Loud people, big boots, frantic children, umbrellas. They are all a potential hazard when you only weigh four pounds!

As you socialize your Chihuahua, always monitor your puppy's body language. When your pup is watching something new, you should be watching your puppy. If at any time your puppy exhibits timid body language, such as dropping his curly tail straight or under his belly, running away, hiding or avoiding the stimulus, shaking, or growling or snapping at the stimulus, you should go into overdrive. Immediately try to distract your puppy with happy talk, doubling the treat rate, or playing, to take his attention off the scary stimulus. If this doesn't immediately relax the puppy, you should remove him to a location where he can relax. Often this is just a few feet away.

Once the pup is relaxed and playing or eating again, you can restart your

approach, going at half the speed you approached before, and stopping halfway there to check in with your pup again. Continue the gradual approach as long as the pup is still happy and relaxed, and retreat a bit when he looks anxious.

If your Chihuahua seems really resistant to approach something, he may need several, or even many, exposures at a distance before he makes it all the way. Do not ever force the puppy to approach something or someone. You can make things much worse and accidentally make him phobic of that particular stimulus for life. If after a few attempts you really are at a loss, or things seem to be getting worse, enlist the help of a professional trainer or behavior consultant.

Out and About: Learning to Travel

As you socialize your puppy you will need to take him out and about to see the world and meet new friends. Trips to the park, to puppy playdates, to the groomer, pet store, or flying across the country on a family vacation are only possible with a well-behaved traveler. Now is the time to introduce him to riding in a carry bag.

Habituating your Chihuahua to traveling in a bag is easy to start right at home. Unzip your carry bag, put it on the floor, and let your pup explore it. If you plan to fly with your Chihuahua, set up an airline-approved soft-sided bag that will fit under the seat in front of you in the cabin. Traveling in the cargo hold is both scary and potentially dangerous for small dogs, so

take advantage of your Chihuahua's small size, and have him travel with you in the cabin of the airplane.

Once you have set up the bag in the house, make it his home away from home. Throw in some treats, give him a stuffed enrichment toy to enjoy, or even feed him some meals in there. Let him sit in it on the couch while you watch TV at night. You want this to be a happy place that your Chihuahua feels secure in.

Make your first few excursions short and fun. A short trip to a friend's house, where there's another puppy to play with is a good start. You want him to enjoy the result of sitting in a carry bag. Most of his initial excursions should be short and pleasurable. After all, if you put him in a bag and then take him somewhere scary, guess who's not going to want to get in the bag next time?

Habituating Your Chihuahua to Husbandry

One of the common pitfalls of inadequate socialization is difficulty handling, bathing, grooming, or restraining your Chihuahua as an adult. Exposure to everyday experiences such as handling, restraint, and grooming until they are no big deal is called habituation. Husbandry, or doggy upkeep experiences, should be included in the initial socialization program, and puppies quickly become habituated as long as you keep initial experiences brief and gentle.

While your new puppy might not be dirty, need his nails clipped or ears cleaned yet, it is critical to introduce those sorts of experiences now. Remember, if you do not practice it now, he may be intimidated and defensive when you try it later. Your priority is to introduce gentle restraint, as well as handling, grooming, and examination of all parts of the body, especially common hot spots such as the head, muzzle, ears, paws, tail, hind end, and around his collar.

Once your pup is enjoying his time in the carry bag, start moving him around in it. Begin in one room by putting him in, giving him a few yummy treats, close the bag, pick it up, and carry him to another room. Put it down, open it up, and put another yummy in the carrier, then move to yet another room.

Move around the house with your Chihuahua riding in the bag. Short, frequent rides will teach him not to worry about moving about in the bag. Once he enjoys these short trips around the house, you are ready to take him out and about the neighborhood.

Grooming and Baths

Baths, and later grooming, can initially be a little intimidating to your Chihuahua puppy. Try breaking it into a series of events, and then work on getting your puppy used to one part at a time. Remember, go at your puppy's pace—you never have to progress through the whole session in one day when introducing new experiences.

First get the puppy used to the towel. Take a small towel and just gently drape it over your puppy while he is sitting on your lap. Immediately give the pup a treat and take off the towel. Play this little game a few times, gradually delaying the amount of time it takes you to give the treat and remove the towel. Soon the puppy is sitting still waiting for the treat, wearing the towel, for twenty-five or thirty seconds at each repetition.

When the pup is ignoring the towel, introduce a little elbow grease by moving the towel around on his back, again working up to patting and rubbing the puppy with the towel for thirty seconds and then offering the treat. If you've done a good job with handling the pup's body from day one, it's relatively straightforward to start rubbing the sensitive spots with the towel, offering a treat after rubbing each little leg, the belly, back, and head.

Gentle grooming can be introduced the same way. Just gently restraining the puppy for thirty seconds, while he eats treats, is often a good start. Then gradually add a little gentle brushing on the body for a few seconds, and offer those yummies. Gently move to more sensitive areas such as the belly, legs, and face.

Don't forget to offer the yummy for each challenging body part! Work up to sessions of grooming that your puppy enjoys for several minutes at a time.

You can, literally, teach a Chihuahua to come running for a grooming session when he sees you take out that brush by making great associations with grooming time.

Nail Clipping

The idea of clipping your new Chihuahua's nails seems to strike fear in the hearts of many otherwise-confident puppy owners, sometimes understandably so. It's a difficult skill to master if you don't practice regularly, and if you're not good at it you will not create a safe and secure experience for your puppy.

Many puppies have had horrible experiences. No one wants to inflict pain on their four-legged friend. So, whenever possible, take time to introduce the process in baby-step increments, making each stage of the game highly rewarding. Just as in previous grooming sessions, the first step is introducing gentle restraint, this time adding the handling and manipulation of the puppy's feet and nails. This may take multiple sessions to master.

Here's the secret to long-term success: If you cannot gently restrain the pup so he's still, and handle all four feet and each individual nail without a rodeo, you should not continue to the next step of cutting his nails. You need to go back a level and continue again, until he patiently tolerates all the funny business with his feet. If that pup is hopping around to evade the restraint, you will hit the nail's nerve and blood supply, and your pup will not let you try that routine a second time.

A good recommendation to new puppy owners is to gently restrain the pup on their lap. As you restrain him, gently lift and squeeze each paw while you feed him a high-value treat. Work up to squeezing each of the paws and each individual nail while the pup stays relaxed. Your goal before you move to the next stage is for the pup to leave his paw in your open hand without pulling it away until you give him the treat.

An alternate technique is to stand up and restrain the pup by gently tucking him under one arm. You will then easily be able to access the front paws, but it may be more difficult to manipulate the back feet. A partner can focus on handling his feet from behind, which is sometimes helpful for puppies that seem more anxious when they can see the clippers coming. Alternately, you can restrain and feed treats while your partner gently moves around and handles each of the feet.

Once this stage is mastered, you can continue. Restrain the pup as you've practiced, hold the pup's paw in your hand and gently tap the nail with the clippers. Immediately pop a treat into your pup's mouth, put her on the ground, and have a rousing bout of her favorite game. Do this with each nail, until she anticipates yummies and fun with the presence of those nail clippers.

When she is calm and relaxed with this process, you can continue to clip the very tip of her itty-bitty nail, careful to stop if the puppy pulls back or shifts position. Again, and more important than ever, get that treat in quickly and proceed to the fun and games portion of the session. If you do one nail a day, or every other day, by the time you clip all sixteen nails, the first nail will be ready to get clipped again. This is better than restraining the puppy for an extended time to get them all clipped in one session and then not doing it again for a month or six weeks.

Continue the "nail-a-day" technique, and add a few strokes of the slicker brush or comb to your daily routine throughout the puppy's first six months. By the end of the first month your pup will handle it like a pro and soon will be dancing in anticipation whenever you pick up your daily grooming tools.

At the Veterinarian's Office

Habituation to basic handling and restraint will go far in making trips to the veterinarian more pleasurable for all involved. Most of the fear and anxiety many dogs have when they are examined or treated by a veterinarian is because the dog was never habituated to restraint and examination. Of course, your Chihuahua is going to struggle and panic when people are holding him down on a scary metal table, poking and prodding.

Going to the veterinarian just for fun should be part of your socialization plan for every new puppy. Your puppy should not just go to the veterinarian for exams and immunizations, as that will very quickly turn your pup into a chicken! Make it a point to drop in just to say hi, and visit frequently enough to establish it as a happy place. Have staff and visitors feed your pup treats while taking a quick peek inside his mouth, looking in his eyes and ears, and holding a stethoscope up to his chest. Just make sure the staff have clean hands and your pup is not placed on the floor or a dirty counter, where he can be exposed to infectious organisms.

You can do your part at home by practicing "examining" all body parts on a frequent basis while you hold him. Start by gently opening your Chihuahua's tiny mouth, checking around for anything out of the ordinary, and popping a yummy right onto his tongue! Continue by looking at each eye, peeking in those ears, running your hands over his body and feet, and peeking under his tail. Make it silly and fun, and habituate your pup to poking and prodding while you gently hold him still.

Your pup should like all this attention and handling. It will make him much more comfortable for those, hopefully, rare times that he really must be treated medically. Many pups will learn to tolerate rather invasive veterinary exams, especially if his previous experience tells him it is going to be quick and yummy.

4 Getting Along with Others: Socializing with Other Dogs

Let's not forget that after socializing your Chihuahua with strange people and children, you are not done. You should make it a priority to safely socialize your puppy with other dogs whenever possible. Remember, if your puppy is not exposed to other dogs on a frequent basis at a young age, he will lose his doggy social skills as an adult, and that is a potential disaster.

Also, a larger dog can accidentally injure such a tiny dog, even when friendly. So carefully monitoring your Chihuahua in the presence of larger dogs is in order. No matter how brave your Chihuahua is, he is on the losing team if he challenges a dog larger than himself.

The Ins and Outs of Dog Parks

Dog parks can be a welcome outlet to a social dog, or a nightmare for a timid or undersocialized dog. Socializing your Chihuahua with other dogs does take some careful consideration and planning, and sometimes a dog park can help you carry out your plan as your puppy gets older.

However, it's never appropriate to bring a puppy that has not completed his immunization series to a dog park. The risk of unvaccinated dogs spreading disease in a dog park is great, and it's almost impossible to know the vaccination status of strange dogs.

If you feel comfortable in trying it with your older puppy, look for a well-designed and sanitary dog park for small dogs. Never bring a Chihuahua into a dog park with large dogs, since a dog any larger than your Chihuahua could easily injure your tiny dog. If you can find an appropriate dog park, it should have plenty of shady spots, enough room and visual barriers such as trees to avoid overcrowding

or bullying, and multiple, double-gated entrances. Take advantage of quiet times to let your dog explore on his own off leash, and always limit playmates to one or two other well-matched puppies his size to play with.

Is That Playmate Safe?

It's not always easy to evaluate if other dogs are appropriate playmates for your Chihuahua, and you should of course err on the side of caution. However, the benefits of careful dog-dog socialization are invaluable.

Finding appropriate playmates for your Chihuahua can be difficult. For example, your tiny four-legged friend may be seen as something more akin to a snack than a dog to some other dogs. Many breeds have been bred to hunt tiny, fast-moving prey items, and your Chihuahua may fit that bill.

Additionally, it's not only large breeds that may be considered predatory. Many breeds not much bigger than your Chihuahua, especially those in the terrier group, are tenacious and proficient hunters and may direct hunting skills toward smaller dogs. So consider the breed, or predominant characteristics, of the potential playmate, as well as size.

How can you tell if it's safe? Always ask if potential playmates have a history of chasing cats or small dogs, or seem overly aroused in the presence of smaller dogs. An overly aroused dog, or a predatory dog, will appear to be intently focused on, or will actively stalk, your small Chihuahua. If you observe predatory behavior or intense chase games that seem to be escalating in intensity, plan to stay on the sidelines with your Chihuahua until a more appropriate match can be made.

Many times, it's just not a good idea to let a tiny Chihuahua play with a much larger dog as it may increase the chance of accidental injury. If your Chihuahua is hiding, looks panicky or intimidated, or you feel uncomfortable with the intensity of the other dog, call the dogs out and end or redirect the play. Of course, there is always an exception to the rule. Some much larger playmates may have a naturally low prey drive, have extensive experience with small dogs, or even live with tiny breeds. Those dogs may know how to "play down" to your Chihuahua's size and play style. Again, it's always a good idea to ask about the previous experience and temperament of potential playmates before getting in over your Chihuahua's head.

Puppy Playdates

Dog-dog socialization is a step in your puppy's development that you should not avoid if at all possible. This is the only time that they can practice their social skills with other dogs. The current American Veterinary Society of Animal Behavior position statement[1] recommends puppies start socialization as early as seven or eight weeks of age. Of course, they should be vaccinated before coming into contact with other dogs.

Once you have scouted out a few potentially appropriate playmates, go

[1]AVSAB Position Statement On Puppy Socialization, 2008. American Veterinary Society of Animal Behavior

ahead and arrange regular play dates. Try to socialize your puppy with playmates of the same age, that are up to date on vaccinations. Playgroups for young puppies should be indoors or in areas that are off-limits to dogs of unknown vaccination history, such as fenced in yards.

You can start a puppy playgroup, and take turns having it in people's homes on at least a weekly basis. Of course, any puppy that is ill should not be taken to play with other puppies until he is feeling better, to minimize cross-contamination.

Socializing your Chihuahua puppy with other dogs should start early and go late. By this I mean that as long as your puppy is healthy, properly vaccinated, and playing with other healthy puppies or dogs, he should start socializing immediately and continue throughout adulthood. If your Chihuahua hardly ever sees other dogs as a pup, it's likely he

will never quite relax in the presence of other dogs as an adult. All his interactions will have that "nervous newbie" quality, and he may become overly aroused around strange dogs.

Observing your puppy's body language during dog play will tell you how enjoyable his interactions are. If the playmate is size and age matched, and the puppies are taking turns being "top dog," with frequent play bows and pauses to sniff, the puppies are probably well matched.

If at any time a puppy becomes panicky, looks out of sorts or intimidated, or is actively hiding behind people or objects, it's time to take a break. It can be a brief one, such as simply redirecting the other puppies in the group away from the pup

that needs some downtime, or play can come to a compete stop and resume later.

Doggy Day Cares

Well-run doggy day cares can be a great help in socializing young dogs for busy pet owners. It can be difficult to put together appropriate play groups on your own, and a day care can provide a great outlet for play, exercise, dog-dog socialization, and all-around boredom busting for teenage or adult Chihuahuas.

A well-run day care will have careful screening of potential clients and will conduct an extensive interview and evaluate your Chihuahua before agreeing to

take your Chihuahua into a playgroup. Dogs should be grouped by size, age, and play style, and have careful supervision of the play groups by trained professionals. Many day-care facilities offer other services including training, grooming, and boarding.

You should never bring your Chihuahua to a facility that does not have a live attendant monitoring dogs at all times in the playroom, as no one would be present to intervene in case of problems. Chihuahuas in particular should not be placed in groups with larger breeds or in play groups with predatory breeds such as terriers.

On-Leash Introductions to Other Dogs

As you take your new Chihuahua out and about, you may have opportunities to practice on-leash introductions to other dogs. Of course, you don't have to approach or say hello to other dogs you don't know, but if you know the other dog is friendly there are some suggestions to keep things safe. On-leash greetings can be awkward, and many dogs become uncomfortable and outright aggressive if their early experiences are intimidating or scary.

Many well-socialized dogs have a similar greeting ritual. Dogs will usually approach at an angle and sniff each other's faces and rear ends or flanks. Try not to interfere in this normal greeting ritual,

and keep your leash loose and untangled. If at any time the dogs freeze or growl, interrupt them by calling your puppy out and then step away, without tugging on the leash if possible. Pulling on the leash can push a frustrated or nervous dog into reacting defensively, often instigating a fight.

Make it a practice to have the puppy check in with you and offer a sit, and when he is calm, give him permission to approach the other dog only if you know the other dog. Keep greetings brief, and remember to call him back to you if the arousal level starts to escalate.

5 Remedial Socialization for Adult Chihuahuas

Sometimes an adult Chihuahua has not benefitted from a comprehensive socialization plan during puppyhood. Many adult Chihuahuas have ended up on the short end of the stick when it comes to getting appropriate exposure to novel stimuli, for a variety of reasons. Sometimes the puppy was in a shelter environment, pet store, or kennel for the duration of his socialization window. Sometimes he was socially isolated in a home environment due to fear of infectious disease, was in a hospital for an extended stay, or because his busy and distracted family just didn't know he should be out and about as a young pup.

The hallmarks of poor socialization in the adult dog are profound shyness or aggression. How can two behaviors that seem polar opposites be symptoms of the same problem? Many dogs will resort to avoidance, or shyness, of new stimuli when they fear it. Remember if a dog has not been exposed to a stimulus to become habituated to it before sixteen weeks old, he will fear it. Sometimes you will see the other end of the spectrum. Often, the dog

has tried avoidance, and it was not successful, so he resorts to aggression in an attempt to drive the scary stimulus away. The best defense is a good offense for many adult, under-socialized Chihuahuas.

So, can we re-socialize an adult Chihuahua that is exhibiting signs of shyness or even aggression? With time, patience, and often professional help, the answer is yes.

Rehabilitating the Adult Rescue Chihuahua

Some adult dogs coming from rescue organizations, in particular puppy mill dogs and dogs that have been raised in pet stores, shelters or kennels until young adulthood, may have serious deficits in their socialization history due to social isolation during puppyhood.

Many of these Chihuahuas are receptive to socialization programs and with some patience and a good re-socialization

plan will habituate to life in your household quite well. Some of these Chihuahuas may have been so socially isolated or mistreated that they are in a chronic state of terror. These dogs are very slow to adapt to home life, they fear any new situation or people, and have difficulty forming any meaningful bonds with humans.

If you have recently adopted an adult Chihuahua from a rescue organization, and he was evaluated, ask to review the results with a shelter trainer or behavior counselor. These results will help direct you in transitioning your Chihuahua into your home, and will help identify any areas that you should target in your socialization and training program. If your recent adoption is a DWI (Dog With

Issues), take advantage of any post-adoption support the rescue organization can offer you. It's critical to follow any recommendations they make regarding transitioning the new Chihuahua into your home to ensure success.

If your Chihuahua has not been evaluated, and you have no behavior history, you should proceed with a socialization plan slowly. While a shy dog may never be a social butterfly you can help him become desensitized and habituate to people, places and things in his new environment. If your Chihuahua is currently aggressing toward people or other dogs, or threatening you directly, you really need to seek the help of a professional to put together a behavior modification plan.

When Do You Need Help?

Whenever your Chihuahua is exhibiting signs of shyness or aggression that are escalating and not resolving, it's important to reach out and seek professional help from a certified professional dog trainer, animal behavior counselor, or veterinary behaviorist. They can provide a full behavior evaluation and then design or recommend behavior modification plans to help your Chihuahua adjust to life in your home.

Some of the more common behavioral difficulties that people need help with include fearful or aggressive behavior toward strange people or dogs either inside or outside the home, anxious behavior when separated from human companions, resource guarding, and noise reactivity. Reactions will seem out of context in the situation: Your Chihuahua is not a little timid around strangers but is suddenly having a full-blown anxiety attack in the presence of every new person that enters the home. Your Chihuahua is not occasionally barky when on leash, but appears ready to tear another dog's head off every time he sees one. These are reactions that have often subtly started under the radar and suddenly seem magnified after a few episodes. A few uncomfortable incidents can snowball into a dog with a bad reputation and an aggression label that may be unjustified.

If you feel like your Chihuahua is reactive and getting worse, don't hesitate to seek professional help immediately. The earlier someone helps you address the issue, the easier it will be to modify or resolve.

Aggression: Is There a Cure?

Behaviorists identify up to fifteen different kinds of aggression in domestic dogs. An important point to remember is that aggressive behavior serves a function to the aggressor and is therefore reinforced when conflict happens and the outcome is in his favor. However, this also means aggressive behaviors can be changed, and more appropriate behaviors can become just as functional to the dog. Some kinds of aggression respond well to behavioral therapy, and some do not. Almost all kinds can be managed to keep people safer.

Some recognized types of aggression are maternal- or hormonally-based aggres-

sion, pain, predation, fear, play, territorial, resource guarding, interdog- or social-status related, redirected and idiopathic, among others. Some of these behaviors are considered "hardwired," meaning they have strong biological function for the well being of the dog and are very resistant to modification. Other kinds of aggression have been learned through experiences that a dog has had and are often more amenable to modification.

One such example of a hardwired aggressive behavior is predatory aggression—it's not directed as a social threat toward others but as a means to food acquisition. Because of this, some researchers don't consider predation as an aggressive behavior, although it looks aggressive to the average person.

Another example of hardwired behavior, maternal aggression, dissipates with changes in hormones when pups are weaned. Similarly, pain aggression can completely resolve when the underlying medical condition is addressed.

Resource guarding, further broken down into food, object, space or location guarding, and people guarding, is an example of aggressive behavior largely learned through experience. For example, if a dog is threatened when he has coveted items or is in his special space, and the dog makes ugly faces with his teeth and growls, and the perceived threat goes away, the ugly face and growling behavior was reinforced and will happen more often. These kinds of aggression can be greatly improved, if not completely resolved, with a modification program. Teaching the dog that there is no threat can be effective.

Certainly, there are typical kinds of aggression that Chihuahuas may show. Sometimes Chihuahuas exhibit fear aggression, which is largely learned and then reinforced by subsequent experience. After unsuccessfully trying to evade the fearful stimulus, such as big, scary strangers or strange dogs approaching them, they resort to acting out aggressively in an attempt to chase it away. To a Chihuahua weighing only six pounds, everything bigger than him is a potential threat.

Resource-guarding behaviors are another common issue. The somewhat stereotypical sight of a Chihuahua snarling at approaching strangers when held by his owner, or staking out territories such as beds or couches in the home that elicit growls and snapping when others approach, are examples of resource-guarding behaviors. Food and toy guarding are other examples of this kind of behavior.

A Chihuahua exhibiting this behavior feels his resource is at risk and is ready to defend it at all costs, so watch out! The good news is that resource guarding is amenable to behavior modification.

The prognosis of solving an aggression problem depends on what kind of aggression your Chihuahua is presenting with, the duration of time the behavior has been exhibited, and client compliance with recommendations and protocols.

If your Chihuahua is exhibiting any kind of aggression, get professional help immediately. With an accurate diagnosis and a well-thought-out modification plan, you may be able to resolve many kinds of aggressive behavior.

6 Great Games for a Happy Chihuahua: Playtime and Environmental Enrichment

Playtime with Your Chihuahua

Play is vital to the health and well-being of your Chihuahua. It helps your Chihuahua develop social skills with other dogs and humans, provides an appropriate outlet for exercise, and provides mental stimulation and enrichment to alleviate boredom. Play is also important in many behavior modification programs and an excellent way to provide reinforcement during training exercises.

How can we define play? Briefly, play behavior is pleasurable, spontaneous activity that allows practice of other behaviors, in and out of context and in a nonthreat-ening manner. Play only occurs when animals are relaxed and stress free, and is repressed when animals are threatened or distressed; it is therefore a helpful indicator of the mental state of an animal.

Though all puppies play, both with other puppies and with people, some adult dogs will become wall flowers if not given a chance to practice their skills during adolescence. Some adult dogs have been so play deprived as youngsters that it can interfere with how they connect on a social level with the humans and other dogs in their life, causing real difficulties in their behavioral health.

Many puppies raised in puppy mills, and later in pet stores, or socially isolated for any reason, will not know how to play well. It pays off to be creative in your approach with these dogs, as they quickly become withdrawn if the play style is intimidating or too intense.

Some of these wall flower dogs may be interested in object play such as fetch; some may respond to gentle physical play such as running or chase games; and some may respond to enrichment-style play with food-dispersal toys. Start off slowly and offer a variety of opportunities for your Chihuahua to feel relaxed while you engage him in gentle, brief play to build up confidence. Your dog may develop a passion for play, and it will enrich his life, as well as yours, as you build a relationship with your Chihuahua.

Great Games

Sometimes play is intuitive: A silly little movement or noise elicits a playful response. Sometimes it's not intuitive: You throw a ball and your Chihuahua just looks at you then walks away.

Each Chihuahua has a play-style preference. Some enjoy objects or toys, some enjoy physical contact and activity, and some enjoy the mental stimulation of interactive toys and puzzles. Many Chihuahuas enjoy chasing or tug games—more on that later. Most dogs will enjoy a variety of play styles at different times, so mix it up and offer games of various play styles in a single play session. Here are a few Chihuahua-approved games to get you started.

Object play often focuses on throwing and retrieving an object such as a ball, stick, or flying disc. Chihuahuas that enjoy this sort of play often develop a preference for one object (my ball!) and will spend hours repeating this game over and over.

Making sure the texture and size of play objects are appropriate for your tiny dog will go far in engaging your Chihuahua in this sort of play. If the object is physically intimidating or hurts (getting hit by a hard rubber ball hurts!), your dog may be turned off. Chihuahuas often do well with objects sized to smaller species, such as squeaky mice or tiny balls with crinkly fabric rather than hard rubber, so don't overlook the cat or ferret toy aisle in your search for that just-right fetch toy.

Some Chihuahuas will enjoy a session of rousing physical activity. Sprinting across the park with your Chihuahua is good

exercise for both of you! Another Chihuahua favorite is the classic "find it" game.
A variation on "find it" is the classic game
of hide and seek. Dogs love it, and everyone knows the game so guests and family
members of all ages can play along.

You can hide objects such as favorite
toys, balls, and treats, or if you have a
partner you can take turns hiding people.
Initially, you may have to teach your
Chihuahua to seek for objects or people
by making it easy.

Leave your Chihuahua in a sit-stay,
have a game partner hold him. Take a
high value treat or favorite toy and place
it somewhere obvious in the room like
under a table, but still highly visible.
Return to your Chihuahua, have the dog
sit, and say "Find it!" in a happy excited
voice. Repeat this ten times, each time
keeping it simple but varying the location
widely around the room.

When your Chihuahua is anticipating
the seeking part, you can start to make the
finds more difficult by hiding them under
another object, higher, such as up on furniture, in bags or boxes, or under pillows or
blankets. Begin hiding the object in closets
or in other rooms, again making it easy
for your Chihuahua to see when he enters
the new area and working up to more
difficult, out of sight spots. Don't be sur-
prised when the dog goes to check the last
location the toy was in. Just remind him
to continue the game when he gets there
and nothing's waiting for him.

To adapt the game to hide and seek
with a person is relatively easy. Once your
Chihuahua knows the "Find it!" game
with toys or treats, you can have a person
participate by holding the treat or toy

and going to hide. Have one person hold
your Chihuahua, or use the opportunity
to practice your sit-stay, while the partner goes to hide. Tell the dog to "Find
_____!" and release him to go seek out
the person holding the toy or treat. The
person hiding can jump-start the process
by calling your Chihuahua the first few
times.

When found, the person that hid then
delivers the treat or plays with the toy,
making a big party out of his success.
After a little practice, the person can hide
without the toys or treats, and just have
the party when the dog find him.

Hide and seek games can be played
both indoors and outdoors in contained
areas, or even on leash around the neighborhood. A variety of organized dog
activities, including nose games, scent
work, tracking and even search and rescue
training are based on the "Find it!" idea,
and many Chihuahuas participate in these
activities.

To Tug or Not?

The appropriateness of tug games is hotly debated among dog trainers. While tug is a universally enjoyed game among dogs, it may not always be the safest game between dogs and humans. Many trainers feel it's fine to play tug, with good rules and structure in place, while others feel it gets the dog overly aroused and out of control.

I'm of the mind that tug games, played safely and with very specific criteria, are fine. Of course, my version of tug is no free-for-all. The dog must exhibit low-arousal behavior such as a quiet sit or down before the game begins and frequently throughout the play session. Most important, if the person tugging with the dog cannot follow the rules laid out for the dog and monitor the arousal level, they cannot play tug with the dog. That may mean tugging is off-limits for children, frail adults, or adults that have a hard time controlling their own arousal levels.

When we do play tug, it is structured and controlled. The dog must never ramp up his arousal beyond a specific point, getting out of control, and must respond to cues for calm behavior with one request. If at any time the game goes into hyper-arousal, play stops and the toy is put away. Just because you have a tiny dog does not mean he can be rude, pushy or obnoxious when playing, snatching at the toy and nipping at you.

What Not to Play

It's not good to practice rough-and-tumble games with your Chihuahua that encourage high arousal. It's too easy to inadvertently reinforce inappropriate behavior such as nipping, jumping, snatching, and scooting away out of reach. It's also easy to injure tiny breeds accidentally with wrestling maneuvers.

It's within reason to set boundaries on types of play you do not want to engage in with your Chihuahua based on your comfort level. One word of caution: make sure that everyone in the household is also adhering to the same play rules.

If some people are playing games that encourage inappropriate behavior, such as jumping, nipping or chasing, or encourage out of control behavior, it will carry over into play with other people that may be at risk of injury. For example, if you are encouraging your Chihuahua to snap at your hands and face in play, and then he snaps at a child's face in play, who's at fault? Certainly not your Chihuahua.

Environmental Enrichment

Environmental enrichment is often one of the most overlooked areas of behavioral health for pets. Enrichment is the process of improving physical and psychological health for animals by drawing out species-appropriate behaviors within the context of their biological needs and natural history. In other words, let your Chihuahua be the dog he was born to be.

Historically, zoos have excelled at providing enrichment programs to captive animals. In fact, for animals to thrive in captivity, providing for their mental health needs is just as important as providing for their basic biological needs, such as food and water. Animals that are under stimulated become frustrated, stressed and eventually become ill. Behavioral researchers have found that providing outlets for normal behavior helps avoid development of abnormal, neurotic, self-destructive or detrimental behavior for all species of animals.

In recent years, dog trainers have brought environmental enrichment to our companion animals. It has become part of a well-rounded program, along with good socialization and basic training, to avoid behavioral difficulties such as frustration, aggression, hyperactivity, stress, depression, and general boredom. In other words, your Chihuahua in your living room would benefit from enrichment just as much as the elephant at the zoo or the dolphin at the aquarium.

Is Enrichment Mental or Physical?

The answer is both, often at the same time! Enrichment can come from a variety of sources and address a variety of needs, both mental and physical.

There are five distinct categories of enrichment: social (relationships with other animals, people, and some objects), cognitive (problem solving, puzzle feeders,

were prototypes from zoos and aquariums that have been introduced to pet owners. You will see things that bounce, roll, squeak, spit out treats, encourage chewing, and smell interesting. However, not everyone has a huge budget to set aside for expensive toys, so creativity is key, and there is an array of other options for do-it-yourselfers.

How Can Enrichment Help You and Your Chihuahua?

The fact is, many doggie behavior problems are a result of boredom combined with a lack of supervision. If you don't provide appropriate enrichment activities for your dog, your Chihuahua may devise his own enrichment sessions, usually by destroying your couch, shoes, kitchen cabinets, or chair legs. Electrical cords, down bedding, and children's toys are also favorite targeted items for many bored puppies.

Although Chihuahuas are a small companion breed they should not be exempt from enrichment activities. They may even need it more than your neighbors large-breed dog, as your Chihuahua is a largely indoor pet that might not get regular outdoor exercise, especially in bad weather. Many of the typical enrichment activities and toys can be adapted to the small breeds.

Dog enrichment toys that are smaller in scale and softer in texture are now marketed to the tiny-breed crowd, and enrichment toys made for pocket pets or cats can be adapted to Chihuahuas. Tiny dogs such as Chihuahuas are more commonly

training sessions), habitat (changes in location and climate), sensory (tactile, visual, auditory, and olfactory stimulation), and food (novel kinds and presentations such as puzzle feeders and dispersal toys). An enrichment session can entail more than one of these categories at a time to provide an endless number of combinations.

A quick walk down the toy aisle of your local pet store will introduce you to the variety of enrichment items now available to the average pet owner. Many of these participating in enriching activities includingas agility, tracking, scent work, and lure coursing. Big dogs don't have all the fun anymore!

Environmental enrichment is worth the investment in both time and money. It's cheaper than replacing chewed-up or broken items that your Chihuahua has gotten busy with. A tiny Chihuahua can take out a pair of expensive sunglasses or mobile phone rather quickly.

Additionally, enrichment sets your Chihuahua up for appropriate boredom busting, which gives you time to get other things done. If your puppy is working on a puzzle feeder, or hunting down rubber food dispensers hidden around the kitchen, you will have the opportunity to return some phone calls, put in the laundry, and help the kids with some homework without monitoring a bored puppy who keeps getting into trouble.

For example, rubber food dispensers can be loaded ahead of time with the dog's meals and refrigerated or frozen. Then, at breakfast, lunch and dinner they can be served up as an activity, either hidden around the house, laid out on the deck, or just turned over directly to the dog. Dry kibble can be spooned into a paper towel roll, the ends twisted closed, and turned into a tug toy that rains kibble when the dog wins. One of the cutest items I've seen are stuff-able, zippered plush toys that can be hidden around the house for a session of hide and seek. Making your Chihuahua use those seek and snack skills is inherently rewarding for him.

Another time of day that would benefit from scheduled enrichment is the evening, just when you are ready to wind down and enjoy some movie time or a good book, or just catch up on paying the bills.

Incorporating Enrichment Into Every Day

Environmental enrichment should be planned ahead of time to be most effective in preventing behavior problems. If possible, an enrichment session or activity every day should be put into effect when a new puppy or adult adoption comes into your home.

One of the easiest ways to attain that is to make meals part of the process. Many trainers never feed their dogs out of a bowl. Instead, they make every mealtime an opportunity to provide an enrichment session.

Your Chihuahua has probably spent much of the day lounging about, waiting for his people to get home to play! You have a hyped-up Chihuahua, who is going to get frustrated and bored quickly if you don't have time to play. Now is the time to set him up with puzzle toys, chews such as bully sticks or pigs' ears cut in half, and rope toys loaded with treats twisted into the loose strands.

Activities, Toys and Recipes for Enrichment

Chihuahuas are particular, and for them presentation is everything. Present them with a too large, too hard rubber toy stuffed with dry kibble, and they'll look at you like you just got off the crazy train. Present your Chihuahua with an appropriately sized, soft textured rubber toy layered with garlic chicken chunks, canned dog food or salmon snacks and bingo, you got yourself a busy Chihuahua. So, the following toys, recipes and activities have been Chihuahua approved to maximize the fun, minimize the effort, and guarantee the safety of your sofa.

You should keep in mind your Chihuahua's basic personality, play style and age when designing an enrichment session. Many Chihuahuas, especially adults, may start out shy or cautious. They will need you to lead them to the toys or will want you to help them interact with a new object. Beginner chewers may need you to stuff toys loosely at first, or may prefer you to smear the initial payoff on the outside of the toy. Don't forget the age of your Chihuahua. Older dogs may approach the session more calmly and slowly and may need a little more time to fully explore the toy options or learn the rules of games compared to younger, more frisky Chihuahuas. Always monitor your Chihuahua with new enrichment toys to make sure they are not choking hazards or potentially dangerous.

The classic enrichment experience is a hollow rubber toy, stuffed with a variety of surprisingly tasty and good-for-your-Chihuahua items. The options of yummies to stuff the toys with are astounding—everything from canned dog food, baby food, peanut butter, to bananas, chopped chicken and vegetables, mashed potatoes, or scrambled eggs and cheese (melted for a few seconds in the microwave and cooled). Rubber toys can also be filled with broth, chunky homemade soup or fruit juice and frozen for the ever-popular "pup-sickles."

For tiny dogs such as Chihuahuas you can offer several smaller toys designed for puppies or soft chewers. As your Chihuahua gets more practiced at un-stuffing toys, you can pack items tighter and into larger, harder rubber toys with challenging segments. Always wash toys after use in hot soapy water, and dry thoroughly before the next use.

A recent addition to the enrichment category is the interactive puzzle toy. Plush puzzle toys stimulate the predatory nature of your pet as he discovers how to remove the squeaker balls or stuffed animals from inside the cavity. Wooden or plastic puzzle toys with moving doors and hidden slots can be loaded with treats to stimulate your Chihuahua's natural desire to problem solve, keeping your Chihuahua engaged and mentally challenged.

Additionally, don't forget the classic standards—bones, edible chew toys and traditional plastic chew toys, often scented or flavored to increase attraction. Not all Chihuahuas are heavy chewers, but for those that are, sterilized bones and chew toys are a satisfying way to spend the afternoon. These sorts of toys should be monitored very carefully so that small pieces are not a choking hazard. If the item is too small for the dog to hold down with his paw, or the whole thing fits in his mouth, he could swallow it.

Another popular enrichment activity that Chihuahuas love are the "chase the mouse" type games. One of my favorites is the remote control rat that you can find in the cat toy section of many pet stores. Chihuahua love to do the pounce and kill maneuver to moving objects. They also will pounce and kill bubbles, sprinklers, and crinkly cat toys on springy poles. Just be careful they don't eat the object once they catch it!

7 Setting Up for Success: Paper, Litter Box, or Outside?

A variety of options are available to the Chihuahua owner for potty time. What works for one family might not be right for another, so decide on a method ahead of time, and make sure you're prepared to tackle it. Don't try to switch between methods, though. It is important to select a method and stick with it, or risk confusing the puppy and lengthening the potty training process.

Successful outdoor potty training requires a suitable spot, where the small dog feels safe and relaxed, and that is convenient to get to in a hurry. Unless you have your own yard, this may be a tall order. The spot selected should be relatively private, with few distractions, and not out in the elements. Don't expect your three pound pup to potty in a windstorm!

Paper or litter box training is an acceptable alternative to outdoor potty training for people who live in hi-rise apartments, for senior citizens or those with limited mobility or difficult access to the outdoors in a hurry. Again, the spot selected should

be quiet and out-of-the-way, but easily accessible when needed.

That Small Dog Sense of Space

It's natural for Chihuahuas to keep their space tidy, both for health reasons and to avoid calling undue attention to their resting space. Initially, mom did this for your puppy by cleaning her up after potty times, but when the litter was mobile, the puppies would potty away from the den or whelping box whenever possible.

Keep in mind that Chihuahua puppies are tiny, and so their resting space is correspondingly small. While your sense of space includes your entire living area, sometimes many rooms on multiple floors, your puppy's space may be the few inches surrounding a sleeping area or crate. Your big space can even be a bit foreign and intimidating for that tiny pup! One of the more challenging aspects of successful potty training is to gradually enlarge the puppy's sense of space to the same size as yours.

Using Crates, Gates, Pens, and Leashes

A puppy crate. Yes, you need one, and no, they are not cruel. Here is your first rule of house-training: When your puppy is not supervised, she is contained.

Dogs naturally seek out safe, small dens where they can rest. Think of a crate as a portable den, or a bed with sides and a roof. This portable den can be for use just in puppyhood, when the world is dangerous to an exploratory puppy, or used throughout the remainder of the dog's years. Many adult Chihuahuas love having

access to their cozy crate, and will choose it over other sleeping spots in the home.

Your Chihuahua will love her crate if it is introduced carefully at a young age. Your Chihuahua's crate should be large enough for her to stand up and turn around in, but still be cozy. A Chihuahua puppy needs the smallest of crates, and if the crate is made of wire your pup may be happier with a towel thrown over it for privacy.

Teaching your puppy to love the crate is often relatively easy. Take the door off, and start by tossing a few yummies or snazzy new toys into the crate. Let your pup enter the crate, sniff out the treats and toys and have a great time. When she is confidently entering and maybe even hanging out in the crate for a few minutes at a time, replace the door and give her a yummy stuffable enrichment toy or stuffed bone, and close the door for a few minutes. Sit in the room, reading a book or watching TV, while she works on that yummy bone. After a minute or two, open the crate and take your pup to the potty area.

After several sessions in the crate for five or so minutes at a time, begin leaving the room while she works on her chew toy. If your pup is a worrier, keep the amount of time brief, maybe just a minute or so. Gradually increase the amount of time the pup will busy himself in the crate while you go about the house doing your chores. Once the pup is comfortable in the crate for longer periods, say thirty minutes or more, you can begin leaving the house for a few minutes at a time.

Baby gates and exercise pens are useful during the house training period, too.

They can be used to section off rooms to keep dogs in, or keep puppies out of other areas of the house, such as upstairs or away from entry areas. Pens are great for keeping puppies in the potty area of a yard, too. Keep in mind that if you are sectioning off entire rooms without access to a potty area, you must supervise the puppy until she has learned to hold it until potty time, which means older puppies only.

What's Your Routine?

There is no one-size-fits-all potty training routine. Every family has different schedules, so success depends on helping your pup adapt to your schedule while setting her up to succeed by meeting her basic needs. Consistency is key, so if your day-to-day activities are unpredictable or irregular, your pup may be confused. It's often helpful to write down and post the puppy's regular routine where everyone can see it and follow along, or even assign regular times to family members to make sure it's a priority. The following are some examples of different types of potty routines.

Method 1: Teaching Your Chihuahua to Potty Outside

First thing in the morning your puppy is bursting! Immediately take her to that quiet location that you previously scouted out for suitability. Your puppy should be leashed and escorted to the potty spot, as puppies get easily distracted and will

"forget" that they had to go. Use a leash or carry your Chihuahua to the potty spot, and no monkey business on the way!

Restrain your pup if she tries to wander off and hasn't attempted elimination. Allow the pup to sniff around as you stand in the potty zone, though, because sniffing usually leads to potty success. You can put down a piece of previously soiled paper and leave it there to encourage the pup to sniff and squat.

Puppy potty time is where the patient owner gets results. Some pups will immediately do their thing, but others may take upwards of five or more minutes to relax enough to empty out. If you've tried the waiting game without any success, don't assume the wee one doesn't have to go, just confine the pup for another fifteen minutes and try again later. It's in there!

Once the puppy is successful, follow up immediately with a high value reward that you have hidden in your pocket and a little off leash playtime before heading back in for breakfast. A word of caution—don't let your puppy learn that you go inside immediately after potty time, or she may learn to hold it to enjoy the outdoors longer.

Offer your puppy food and water on a schedule recommended by your veterinarian. It's usually better not to leave food out all day, because if your pup is nibbling all day, she will be dribbling all day! Of course, consult your veterinarian if your Chihuahua is very tiny or has a health issue for specific recommendations on feeding schedules, since small dogs may be at risk for low blood sugar.

After each meal, confine the puppy for a few minutes to let that digestive system get to work but watch closely; at the first sign of the "potty dance," or any sort of unease or distractedness, it's time to head back outside to the potty spot. Some puppies will need to head back outside immediately after eating, and some may need to ruminate a little longer, until fifteen or twenty minutes later, bingo! Time to potty!

If your pup is successful during the after meal potty run, she can play off leash while supervised. Use this time to introduce her to increasing areas of the home, since you know she's empty for a while. If not truly successful on this potty run, it might be a good idea to place her back in the crate for another, maybe shorter, confinement period and have another opportunity later. Every pup will have a different body schedule, but if the pup is eating, exercising and brought to the potty spot on a very regular schedule, say every thirty to sixty minutes while awake, the schedule should become regular.

When the family is leaving the house for work and school, have a final potty run, put your pup in her confinement area, give her a distraction, and keep goodbyes low key. Very young pups, up to four months old, should have someone coming in to potty them every three hours. Pups older than four months can be gradually accustomed to a less frequent schedule, but should not be crated longer than about four hours at the most. While crates can be a great tool, if your pup is forced to potty in it because you were gone too long, it will be useless.

Repeat the potty routine after every meal, and after sleeping, playing, and before bed. For very young pups, this may need to be repeated every thirty minutes, gradually increasing the time to several hours at a time as the pup gets older. Use the periods after successful potty trips to introduce the pup to gradually expanded areas of your living space, while supervised or on leash.

If the room you're in has a door, close it, or use a portable baby gate as a temporary boundary. Bring the pup's bed or belongings room to room to help her establish those areas as hers, too. Remember, if it's not a bed, it's a toilet, so establish each new area as her "bed."

If the pup regresses or has accidents, decrease her freedom and increase your supervision. Use those mistakes as an opportunity to interrupt your pup during the act by startling her (not too scary, just a hand clap will do), and then redirect her to the right location. Think of it as a learning experience, and make it a point to tighten up your supervision. You have gone too fast, and your pup will need to spend more time honing her skills before she can be trusted loose in the house.

Method 2: Teaching Your Chihuahua to Potty on Paper or in a Litter Box

Paper or litter-box training can be the ideal solution for Chihuahua. Puppy pads are readily available, and will absorb the urine, making it easy to dispose of. Litter-box training has also becoming much more common for small dogs and can be used much like a cat litter box. The puppy pad or litter box should placed in an area that makes the puppy feel secure and relaxed enough to potty easily.

Paper or litter-box training is similar to outdoor potty training, except that instead of going to an outdoor potty spot, you are taking the puppy to an indoor potty spot. Paper training is not just putting down paper all over the house to contain the mess. If you put down paper

everywhere, your puppy will pee everywhere. It will slow down the learning process, and your Chihuahua may never be completely house-trained. It's important to teach the pup to hold it until given the opportunity to access the paper. This, means keeping a schedule just as rigorous as for outdoor training.

Pick an area of the house where it would be convenient to set up a potty spot. A kitchen corner or laundry room is often chosen because of easy cleanup. Set up a pen, and line it completely with paper or place the litter box in the pen. The potty area should be small, giving the puppy no choice about where to potty.

Follow the schedule as described above in method 1, but instead of taking the puppy to an outdoor potty location, place her in the potty pen. Just as above, reward

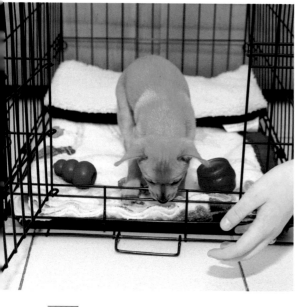

her for success, and then let her out for supervised play.

After meals briefly confine the pup in her crate until it is potty time again. After five or ten minutes, bring the puppy to the potty pen, praising for success. Place the puppy in the potty pen every thirty to sixty minutes, as well as after playing with toys, getting some exercise, and sleeping, gradually increasing the amount of time between potty trips.

Once the puppy has emptied out successfully in the pen on the paper, let the pup explore the room. Again, this should be either done on leash or with 100-percent supervision in case the pup makes a mistake and you have to redirect her.

After several weeks of successful elimination on paper or litter the dog should begin to seek out that substance to eliminate. Once the pup is keeping the rest of the pen clean and eliminating only on the paper or in the litter box, you can then attempt to enlarge the pen and move the paper. You want to move the paper around the room so that the puppy doesn't form a location preference, meaning the pup can only potty in that location. You want the pup to seek the paper to potty on, not the location, just in case you need to move it at a later time.

Slowly increase the size of the pen, and then begin to give the pup access to the the whole room while still seeking out her potty spot to eliminate. Over a period of weeks or months, increase the pup's freedom to include the whole house. If at any time the puppy is having accidents, you must increase your supervision while decreasing the puppy's freedom to new areas.

Cleanup Duty

 Mistakes are going to happen, and how you handle them will keep your potty training moving forward. If you catch a mistake midstream, interrupt with a soft clap of the hands or a gentle "oops!", and redirect the puppy to the appropriate spot. By using punishment carefully, you will teach the puppy to avoid eliminating in front of you if you gently scare her during potty time. If your pup already made a mistake, you weren't paying attention, and the responsibility was yours to keep things on track.

Enzymatic clean up products are the most effective for removing animal odors but must be used in sufficient quantities to remove all scent. That usually means completely saturating the area, including the padding under any carpeting, and letting it air-dry. Messes should be soaked up with paper towels and hot water if needed before application of the enzymatic cleaner. Avoid use of ammonia-based cleaners, which will leave a urine-like scent in the spot. Other cleaning products, disinfectants, and compounds already present in the area also easily denature the enzymes, so no soap

or solutions should be used before application. A diluted solution of vinegar and water is a good odor-masking remedy for areas outdoors such as decks and patios.

Quick Potty Training Checklist

- Crate or pen the puppy when not supervised
- Take the puppy to the potty area:
  - Upon awakening
  - After playing
  - Five to ten minutes after eating anything (including bones, treats and toys)
  - Every thirty to sixty minutes during the day
  - Just before bedtime
- Establish regular meal schedules
- Use crates, gates, or pens, to restrict the puppy's access to inappropriate areas of the house, especially carpeted areas
  - Carry or walk the puppy on leash to the potty area
    - Allow the pup to sniff, but no playing until her business is done
      - Play with or walk the puppy after potty time if it was successful
      - Don't punish accidents harshly; gently interrupt with a soft hand clap
  - Use enzymatic cleaners

57

Is Potty Training Always a Training Issue?

Sometimes potty training takes a turn for the worse in an older or adult Chihuahua. This can happen for a variety of reasons.

Older male puppies and young adults may start to mark territory in and around the home. This is normal behavior for intact male dogs, as well as some neutered males and females. Let's face it, dogs can be territorial and like to leave a little "pee mail" for others to investigate, so it may seem a

no-brainer for a Chihuahua becoming an adult to advertise he is available. When this is happening indoors, however, it's a real glitch in the house-training process.

If you notice your older pup or adult is having more accidents, pay attention to when and where they are occurring. If accidents are increasing when other dogs are nearby, and are on the vertical surfaces of furniture or walls (or in bedding or in front of windows for the marking females), you may have territorial marking. This can be difficult to correct if not caught early.

However, if you are really on top of things, you can increase your supervision and restrict access to those areas that your Chihuahua is marking to keep it to a minimum. It's also not uncommon to have intact male Chihuahuas wear a belly band, a sort of absorbent belt the dog wears around his midsection. The marking doesn't really stop, but the belly band absorbs the urine and keeps your house tidy.

When any previously well potty-trained Chihuahua has a sudden and significant relapse, medical causes should always be ruled out before assuming it's behavioral. In fact, many behavior consultants will not see the dog until they have had a complete physical exam to rule out medical conditions. Most commonly, the dog has an infection of the urinary tract or kidneys, resulting in increased frequency and straining, with blood sometimes seen in the urine. Metabolic disease such as diabetes or Cushing's syndrome may have your Chihuahua urinating more, and older dogs may be subject to canine cognitive dysfunction, or old-dog senility, that make them forget their previous good manners.

Retraining the Adult Chihuahua

Retraining the adult Chihuahua, whether a rescue or a dog that has become un-house-trained due to poor supervision often requires some backtracking to ensure success. It's important to set your Chihuahua up for success, and expect confusion and mistakes for the first few days if the dog is in a new environment.

Just like for the youngsters, it's important to restrict the dog's access to new areas by using crates, gates, pens or tethers for the first few weeks. This will prevent accidents. You can always relax your routine later, but it is difficult to address bad habits after they're established. Think problem prevention and good habits, rather than fixing things after they are off track.

Over the first few weeks, set up the schedule for your adult Chihuahua carefully. For example, besides first thing in the morning, after eating, and before bed, add a few extra trips to the potty spot every one to two hours throughout the day. Make sure you reward those potty trips, too, and just like the pups, make sure you go to the same spot every trip to make it clear to your dog that there is a specific place to do her business, and it's not inside. Use that time after successful potty trips to introduce your new Chihuahua to expanded areas of the home under close supervision.

If your new Chihuahua seems a bit inhibited during potty time, pay attention to the surface and place of the potty spot selected. It's possible your adult Chihuahua prefers one substrate or another, so try out grass, as well as cement, dirt and maybe even paper. The potty spot should be quiet and distraction free as well.

If you catch your new Chihuahua in the act, remember to gently interrupt the chain of events, and hustle her off to the right spot. When she's successful in the new potty spot remember to reward that effort on her part.

If your new Chihuahua has an accident or two during her first days home, remember, dogs don't generalize behaviors to new environments well. Maybe she knew not to potty in her previous home, but for all she knows now the rules may be different here—this is not an unusual assumption for a dog to make. Give her the benefit of a refresher course over the next few weeks, and she will get back on track.

8 *The Fundamentals of Training*

Sometimes when people see a book about training Chihuahuas they snicker or giggle. They don't always seem to take training small dogs seriously. After all, how much trouble could a six-pound Chihuahua get into, so why all that effort to train him?

The first reason is for his safety. If your Chihuahua is uncontrollable, especially in public, he is in danger. What would happen if you opened your car door in a busy parking lot, your Chihuahua launched out into the mayhem, and you had absolutely no recall training under your belt?

Another important reason is for other people's safety. If your Chihuahua is snarly and aggressive out of fear, anyone reaching to pet him is at risk for a nip. Small dogs hurt when they bite too, and a bite directed at your face, or that of a well-meaning child's, can be dangerous.

A trained Chihuahua is happier, too. Too many dogs go through life worried in unfamiliar situations because they don't know what to do. Your dog will appreciate it when you direct his behavior, but if you have not taught your Chihuahua any skills, how can you tell him what to do? Often, the little Chihuahua is shy, nervous,

or hyperactive, and his human is frustrated and embarrassed by his resulting behavior.

Mostly, we train because it's fun. Nothing brings out the human-animal bond like a relationship built on trust and good communication, and positive-reinforcement training is the way to get there.

How to Find a Training Program

When new Chihuahua owners think about training their puppy, the first thing they think about is a group obedience class. Though that may be good for some puppies for a variety of reasons, you have some other options that might be better.

The best way to start will be to find a good teacher or school. You should look for a trainer who uses positive-reinforcement methods, and ask to observe a class. Many trainers will offer classes for just small dogs. Even if the students are not using clickers, they should be recognizing good behavior and reinforcing it. Stay away from teachers who are punishing or aggressively correcting behavior.

Watch the students and their dogs closely. While learning is hard work, the instructor should be introducing material in a way that keeps the dogs happy, relaxed, and successful. If the dogs are worried, the handlers are stressed, and the instructor is not able to adjust the material to the team's level of understanding, from beginner to advanced, keep looking.

Another thing to avoid is a teacher that encourages the use of aversive punishment or other harsh treatment. If you see dogs with choke chains, lots of yelling and "corrections," and the teacher is intimidating dogs or people, keep shopping. If instructors don't believe in training with treats or other rewards, again, shop elsewhere, because they don't understand learning theory or positive reinforcement training. Most importantly, if you feel uncomfortable about how an instructor is interacting with your Chihuahua, stop and ask questions. Don't let someone bully you or your Chihuahua.

Many instructors offer group classes for beginning students. Sometimes, however, it's difficult for novice trainers to concentrate in the chaos of a class with too many puppies, and you can quickly become frustrated and overwhelmed.

Instead, look for a teacher than offers a combination of private and group lessons. For example, a few private lessons in your home can get you up and running with some basic skills, while going to a group lesson or playgroup will help with your pup's socialization skills. A group class that meets outdoors, but keeps the material simple, can help you learn to generalize new skills that you've mastered in a private lesson.

If you do attend a puppy kindergarten-style training class, expect that most of the training will be done at home with little supervision. The classes are really to demonstrate the homework and troubleshoot what you worked on the week before. If at any time you don't understand the material or you're having difficulty, approach the instructor and ask for some one-on-one assistance. After all, instructors want you to succeed, too!

How Dogs Really Learn

There are many mistaken assumptions about how dogs learn: It's all in the voice (usually, deep, loud, and booming); you need to show em' who's boss (by rolling them on their back to make them submit); endless repetitions (often with "corrections" for wrong behavior); old dogs can't learn new tricks; and so on.

The truth is, dogs learn just like all other mammals. There's no magic involved, and it doesn't require any whispering. Anyone can learn the basic principles, and use them to affect their Chihuahua's behavior. The basic principles include classical conditioning, sometimes called Pavlovian or respondent conditioning, and operant conditioning.

Briefly, classical conditioning is the pairing of a neutral stimulus in the environment with an unconscious response. The important part is that it occurs without the animal knowing.

The classic example is Pavlov's dogs drooling, the unconscious response, being paired with the bell, the neutral stimulus. Nobody trained the dogs' response, but when the kennel attendant opened the door, ringing the attached bell, the event was always immediately followed with food. Pairing occurred, and quickly the bell meant food was coming, leading to the hungry dogs drooling.

Classical conditioning regularly happens in your Chihuahua's environment, and affects the resulting behavior. The leash, previously a neutral stimulus, is quickly associated with walk time. Soon, just picking up the leash will elicit running to the door, tail wagging, and barking. The sound of the car in the driveway means Mom is home, so your Chihuahua waits at the door. The word "cookie" signals a tasty treat is coming, resulting in a happy Chihuahua racing to the kitchen ahead of you. The sight of those towels and toenail clippers means a not-so-fun grooming session is on the horizon (quick, hide under the bed).

Operant conditioning is at work when the dog offers a conscious behavior, and learns from the consequences, either positive or negative. An everyday illustration of operant conditioning involves training your Chihuahua to "shake" on command. When your Chihuahua picks up one of his forepaws a bit (operant response), give your Chihuahua a tasty treat (positive reinforcer). That reward will increase the probability that the operant behavior will occur again. If you pinched his paw to punish him for raising it, it would decrease the probability that he would repeat that behavior. Of course, there's quite a few reasons you should not punish him for offering behavior (more on that later).

Harness Operant Conditioning

Modern trainers have a set of tools at their disposal that avoid the old-fashioned "yank and jerk" methodology of the past. Not only are dogs and their trainers happier in the process of training but dogs are achieving fluency of behavior unheard of using the old intimidation methods. Operant conditioning, first described in the laboratory by behaviorists studying behavior in rats and pigeons as a model for human learning, has been a revelation for animal trainers, and dogs have reaped the benefits.

Throughout the following chapters I will refer repeatedly to "clicker training." Clicker training is a term describing operant conditioning using the principles of positive reinforcement (rewarding behaviors we do like to make them occur more frequently), sometimes negative punishment (withholding rewards for behaviors we don't like to make them occur less frequently), and extinction (ignoring behaviors we don't like until they are no longer offered). It's a mindset as well, in that clicker trainers shun the use of aversive punishment, force or intimidation methods.

Why do we use a clicker? Dog trainers commonly use a toy clicker to "mark" the particular behavior the dog should repeat in order to get reinforcement or reward, hence the name clicker training. Marking the behavior with sound (CLICK!), followed immediately with a high-value reward, helps the dog process precise information quickly, and speeds up the training process. Other behavior markers such as a voice signal can be used, but a clicker stands out well against environmental noise. Once the specific behavior is offered freely, it is then placed on cue by the trainer to have it under stimulus control.

Behavioral research tells us that positive reinforcement of a behavior makes it likely the dog will repeat the desired behavior. Trainers who apply these principles of operant conditioning can communicate their intent to the dog, and it becomes the basis of a training language that both human and dog can understand. Positive reinforcement of good behavior becomes the foundation of a great dog-human relationship and is always a win-win situation.

Understanding Reward and Punishment Scientifically

Reward and punishment are two strongly charged words in our society. They have all kinds of connotations and mean vastly different things to different people. Being served a plate of broccoli is rewarding to some of us but is a strong punishment to others. Access to the snowy backyard is tremendously rewarding for the Samoyed that loves the cold outdoors, but this would be a punisher for the twelve-pound terrier that would prefer to bask in the sun in 90-degree heat. Our perceptions of which consequences are rewarding and which are punishing often interfere with our attempts at changing the behavior of our dogs.

To use operant conditioning successfully, you must step away from what you currently think these two principles mean, and look at them through the lens of a behaviorist. Let's define the terms "reinforcement" and "punishment" scientifically.

What we commonly refer to as a reward is more accurately called a reinforcer. Reinforcers are consequences that make the behavior immediately preceding them increase in frequency. It does not mean the consequence is always good. Here's where it gets tricky: There are both positive and negative reinforcers. Positive means adding something, and negative means taking away something to affect the behavior preceding it.

Positive reinforcers are the "rewards" we all know about. They are the good consequences that are added to make the behavior repeat, such as giving your Chihuahua a treat for sitting. Positive reinforcers can be anything the learner likes, including food, toys, attention, access to environments, or an opportunity to do other behaviors (more on that later).

Negative reinforcers also make the behavior increase in frequency but by removal of a negative stimulus. See, this also gets tricky. A classic example is using an ear pinch to teach the dog to take a retrieval object. The trainer would pinch the dog's ear, a rather harsh technique, until the dog opened his mouth and accepted the object. The pinching would only stop when the dog was successfully picking up the object. Ouch! Clicker trainers stay away from this kind of methodology.

Punishment must be all bad, right? Not so fast. Punishment refers to the effect on behavior, not to how aversive the stimulus is. Punishment decreases the frequency of the behavior immediately before it. Just like in reinforcement, there's positive and negative punishment.

Positive punishment refers to adding a stimulus to decrease the behavior preceding it. The consequence is frequently aversive, otherwise it would be ineffective, and can be harsh or painful. For example, "collar corrections" as a consequence for leash pulling can decrease the incidence of leash pulling. Shocking a dog for crossing a fence line or barking is another rather common positive punisher. Of course, positive punishment often hurts or scares the dog and can also increase aggression when applied to a frightened, confused dog.

Negative punishers can have the same effect, namely, decreasing the incidence of behavior, but these punishers rely on withholding or taking away access to a positive consequence. Withholding petting and attention is helpful in decreasing jumping, without the harmful side effects of stepping on their toes. Stopping play with a too-mouthy puppy is effective in getting the nipping to decrease, saving your fingers. Negative punishers avoid the problem of associating painful consequences with the trainer, while decreasing or stopping unwanted behaviors.

Extinction is another helpful tool for trainers. Extinction relies on stopping reinforcement for a behavior that was previously reinforced and is often a good alternative to punishment. It's often used in combination with the positive reinforcement of an alternate behavior.

In application, you would ignore behavior you don't want and wait for the dog to stop offering the behavior, while selecting something else for reinforcement. For example, to extinguish barking for attention, you would ignore any barking, waiting for and then reinforcing quiet behavior. Extinction may take some time, and extinguished behavior can be subject to spontaneous recovery, but it can be an effective and reliable technique.

The Premack Principle: Let's Make a Deal

Clicker trainers have an ongoing contract with their dogs. The trainer cues the behavior, the dog does the behavior, the trainers reward the behavior. Everybody wins when they follow the rules of the contract. But what if you don't have a clicker and treats, and you want to reinforce good behavior as it occurs in the real world, not just a training session?

Using the opportunity to do another, preferred behavior, is called the Premack Principle, and it can be a powerful method to reinforce a previous behavior. Dog trainers make use of this principle all the time by delivering environmental rewards.

For example, a powerful reinforcer for a dog responding to a recall when chasing a squirrel is to be released back to chasing that squirrel, now that the squirrel has a good head start. Throwing a second ball is a reinforcer for bringing the first one back. Barking once at the back door to go out, rather than scratching it, gets the door opened to the wonderful world of the backyard.

Trainers are also applying the Premack Principle when they back-chain a complex series of behaviors. Each behavior reinforces the previous one, until the behavior at the end of the chain is rewarded with a

primary reinforcer of considerable value. Continuing to the next jump on the agility course is the reward for hitting the contact zone on the dog walk. Running through the tunnel is a reinforcer for taking the correct signaled jump. The next behavior in the chain is a reinforcer for the previous behavior.

Treats Don't Spoil Dogs, Owners Do

Using clicker training, then, seems to make sense, and many people would agree that rewarding a behavior makes it more likely to recur. Of course, some people immediately question the validity of the method, especially the delivery of food as reinforcement.

Doesn't it spoil your Chihuahua to just give him treats all the time? Doesn't clicker training result in a dog that just does what he wants, in hopes of getting a payoff? Isn't it cheating to just give your Chihuahua food all the time? Shouldn't he do things because you told him to, or because he wants to please you?

The answer to all of these questions is no. What spoils dogs is owners giving them treats for behavior they don't want to be repeated. If you make the reward, whatever it is, contingent on the behavior, it is rewarding the behavior that occurred, good or bad.

If you reward jumping with attention, you will get jumping. If instead you wait for your Chihuahua to stop jumping and then reward sitting when it's offered, you're rewarding the sitting. You get what you train, whether you wanted it or not. It's up to you to select appropriate behaviors to maintain, because to your Chihuahua they are both just fine. It's the attention the dog wanted, and he doesn't really care how he gets it.

Many people do just the opposite. They hold up a treat, beg or order the dog to do a behavior, and then give the dog the treat even it he didn't do the behavior. That is bribery, and wishful thinking, not dog training. The dog was rewarded for non-compliance, is still untrained or even more confused, and the owner is frustrated. Everyone loses.

The second question is a little more subtle. Yes, clicker-trained dogs offer a lot more behaviors. They often have many behaviors to offer, and if the behavior offered is not "finished" or under the trainer's stimulus control, the dog may throw it out there to make you click. I can often tell if a dog has been traditionally trained, because of an absence of offered behavior. The dog just sits there, requiring me to lure or prompt him into behaviors. Sadly, these dogs don't take part in the learning process, they learn by rote or to avoid negative consequences.

Accomplished trainers don't consider offering behaviors a detriment to the training process. In fact, the more adept the dog is at throwing behaviors to get clicked, the more you have to choose from to shape what you want. Get the behavior under stimulus control by putting it on cue, and stop reinforcing it if you haven't cued it. The dog will stop offering it off cue, and the problem is solved.

The last questions, regarding food as cheating but petting or praise as the only appropriate reward for dogs, is completely ridiculous. The trainer does not get to pass judgment on what is an appropriate reinforcement for a dog's behavior, only the dog can decide that. Reinforcers and punishers must be relevant to the learner to affect behavior.

Often, owners are confused when a dog's reinforcers are not what they thought they were. I hear "this dog works for petting, he doesn't take treats" all the time. So, I ask the student to complete a fun, active, and easy exercise, and reinforce the dog's compliance with petting. I use this opportunity to point out that sometimes the dog avoids their petting. Often the dog is ducking the owners hand at this stage, and would much prefer to continue the activity than to stop and allow petting. This dog would prefer delivery of an active reinforcer like tugging, or a tidbit of high-value food like hot dogs or chopped chicken, and then get back to training.

When people have this bias regarding using food for training, it is important to remember that every dog, just like people, has his own reinforcers. Sometimes it will be food, but it can also be play, petting, praise and attention, the opportunity to engage in other behaviors, or anything else the dog wants. A good trainer makes learning fun and exciting by using all the reinforcers at his disposal, not just treats. If you're hung up about using food, find something else that works. Just make sure it's relevant to the dog.

Keep It Short

What's almost as important as keeping the reinforcer relevant to the learner is the timing with which it's delivered. In dog training, timing is everything! It's the timing of the click, and subsequent delivery of the reinforcer after that that makes it relevant to your Chihuahua in the training process.

Delivery of a reinforcer should be quick, within a few seconds, for your Chihuahua to understand which behavior to repeat. The dog must be aware of what's being reinforced to repeat it. If you ask your Chihuahua to sit, but deliver the food when he's already popped up, what are you reinforcing? Popping up. You must deliver reinforcement immediately after the dog sits, not too late.

This is why behavior markers such as clickers are so important. They allow you to mark the precise behavior you like and then bridge that marker to the reinforcement that follows a moment later.

Behavior markers like clickers also allow you to introduce distance into your training. Even if you can successfully rely on quick, accurate delivery of a reinforcer when working within a few feet of your Chihuahua, you will find it incredibly difficult once you try to deliver reinforcement from further away. You just can't move fast enough to capture behavior as it happens when you are across the room or on an agility course. Clicking will buy you those few moments, linking the marked behavior to a reinforcer that arrives in the next moment. You can click that sit and then cross the room to deliver the treat.

My Dog Is Not a Dolphin!

Some say that maybe operant conditioning and clicker training is good for lab animals like rats and for dolphins learning fancy tricks for shows, but it doesn't apply to the real world of training manners for pets, working with aggressive dogs, or for training working dogs or serious competition dogs. After all, dogs are not dolphins in a tank, swimming in circles.

Remember that operant conditioning and clicker training has been successfully applied to well over one hundred different species, from humans to cockroaches. Trained behaviors range from simple to incredibly elaborate, including the current United States Navy's use of free-ranging dolphins to detect underwater mines in the Persian Gulf and other areas.

It is true, your Chihuahua is not a dolphin. Your Chihuahua will probably never have to work to that level of expertise, with that independence, and with so many fluent behaviors under his belt. Whatever your Chihuahua training goals might be, from having a nicely behaved family companion to a competitive athlete, clicker training will get you there.

Appropriate Equipment

One of the first things new students ask is "what equipment do I need when I come to a class?" My answer: a dog, a clicker, and some treats. Really, people get way too hung up about having the right kind of collar, the newest, fanciest leash, and the perfect equipment to help them train their dog. I get catalogs with pages of "training equipment" listed, all promising to make dog training magically simple. Forget all that stuff, the tool you really need is your brain. If you don't know what you're trying to do, the perfect collar is not going to help you.

That being said, here are some recommendations to make your life easier on the management end, while you train all those behaviors you plan to work on. For starters, a lightweight collar for identification tags is a good idea. You have a few options for material, including nylon, cotton, or leather.

The lightweight collar should be comfortable, not falling off, but not too tight. You need to check the fit often on a growing pup. It's too big if you can fit more than two fingers between the collar and your Chihuahua's neck, and too small if you can't get two fingers in.

If you have the buckle collar fitting correctly, and it can be pulled over your Chihuahua's head you should use a martingale collar. These are designed for dogs that have a slightly wider neck than the width of his head. Often these are referred to as "Greyhound" collars, because of their popularity with narrow-headed sight-hound type breeds. These collars look like a figure eight, with your Chihuahua's head in one loop, and the leash attached to the other. The are comfy, often padded, and only tightens down when the leash is pulled. They are safe and effective at preventing accidental evasive mishaps, but should not be left on a dog unattended, as the leash loop may be loose enough to get caught on something, causing a choking hazard.

Another way to manage your Chihuahua safely on the street is a body harness. This is a very popular choice with Chihuahua owners, since it takes all the pressure off the dog's delicate neck, avoiding potential injuries to their delicate trachea or the vertebrae of such a small breed. It must fit correctly, however, to prevent your Chihuahua escaping. A preference is for a harness designed with the leash attachment to a ring on the front of the chest strap. This style is helpful since it doesn't let the dog pull forward and learn to tug on the leash.

A lightweight six-foot leash is a good idea, too, so Fido doesn't wander off into traffic. A standard leash for a small dog is one-half inch in width, strong enough to be useful but narrow enough to be comfortable in your hand. Make sure the hardware is appropriately sized; you don't want your Chihuahua getting bumped in the face by a heavy snap. I don't recommend the use of the retractable type leashes. These leashes lend little control, are bulky to hold and use well, and contribute to pulling.

69

9 Applying the Basics of Positive-Reinforcement Training

Understanding how to apply the principles of operant conditioning to training your Chihuahua can be overwhelming when you just want a well behaved, well adjusted companion. Not everyone wants to master an entire scientific discipline, they just want a pet they can live with. With that in mind, the following basic principles can address most issues that will come up when you are working with the average Chihuahua.

Stay Away from "No!"—Build Better Behavior Through "Yes!"

One concept that is difficult for people to master is to stay away from using the word "no!" We say it all the time to each other, and humans are great at making those sorts of extrapolations. NO really doesn't give the dog any relevant information other than "punishment is coming," but it doesn't tell the dog what to do to avoid punishment.

When a Chihuahua is engaged in a behavior that we disapprove of, maybe digging a hole in the middle of your newly planted flower garden, most people's immediate reflex is to yell "NO." Clearly you are unhappy with something about his activity.

At that point the dog has to make an inference about the meaning of the yelling, as he may be engaged in a variety of behaviors at once and has no idea which of those you're trying to interrupt and probably about to punish him for. Most of the time, the inference your Chihuahua makes is not the one you meant.

So, as that dog is excavating the backyard, he is looking at the ground as you approach him, maybe excitedly wagging his tail and barking, just having a generally good time. He may mistake your verbal correction "No!" to mean "Oh, don't dig when humans are approaching or present in the yard," so he politely waits until you have vacated the premises to engage in his dirt party. Not exactly the effect you were looking for.

Now you come back and interrupt him with another "No!" He makes another assessment of the situation and decides perhaps he should dig quietly and, of course, after you have left the premises. Now you have the stealth digger, and he is only following your directions about how and when to dig. The directions you gave him were vague and ineffectual. How can you fault him?

Instead, the more effective, and certainly quicker method, would be to provide an opportunity to say "yes!" by providing an appropriate outlet and then rewarding your Chihuahua for digging the right way. When Fido launches into dirt mode, take him to a preselected spot, encourage him to dig, and even join in the fun. Maybe bury a few toys in there to surprise him when he hits gold!

When you supervise the digging location, and let him dig as a reward for doing it in the right location, he will quickly understand to limit his digging to those areas you've told him are appropriate. You can provide locations both in the yard or on a deck or patio by filling a plastic kiddie pool with sand or potting soil. You can even put the digging activity on cue, and then ask the dog to repeat that behavior

in areas you need a little assistance with when doing your spring planting.

Good dog trainers become expert at providing opportunities to say yes and provide reinforcement for behavior we like, and avoid saying no at all costs. This idea is fundamental to positive-reinforcement dog training and is easy to quickly put into your training methodology.

By using this approach, we learn to say yes to sitting when greeting friends, instead of no to jumping on them. We say yes to quietly laying down in the kitchen during meals, rather than no to counter surfing or begging at the table. We say yes to quietly watching other dogs walk by on the street, rather than no to barking at them. We say yes to walking with a loose leash, instead of no to pulling like a sled dog. We say yes to lying on a dog bed or mat, instead of no to jumping on the couch with muddy feet. It's so much easier to tell the dog what he should do and when he should do it, rather than try to fix the multitude of ways he can get it wrong.

Reinforcers: What Works for Your Chihuahua?

Reinforcement is a consequence that follows behavior, which strengthens or increases the occurrence of that behavior. While there are different kinds of reinforcement, both positive and negative, for our purposes we will restrict our discussion to using positive reinforcement, or rewards, to strengthen and maintain behaviors you would like your Chihuahua to repeat. Negative reinforcement is difficult to apply humanely and should be restricted to use by professionals under very specific circumstances if at all.

Reinforcers can be further broken down into primary and secondary reinforcers. Primary reinforcers, for all species, are related to biology, and require no conditioning to establish. Primary reinforcers include food, food acquisition behaviors such as hard-wired predatory behaviors, water, and access to reproductive activities. Secondary, or conditioned, reinforcers are initially neutral and their value is learned by context when linked to some primary reinforcement.

A good analogy to help pet owners, especially parents, to understand primary and secondary reinforcement is candy and money. Candy is a high-value food reinforcer for most kids, and money is the conditioned reinforcer that gives you access to the candy. Money is initially neutral to kids—give a toddler a dollar, and he will scribble on it. Show an older kid that money buys candy a few times, and suddenly money has tremendous value. It is saved, counted, and can be used as a conditioned reinforcer for behavior you want repeated, such as taking out the trash. It has been linked to the candy reinforcer strongly enough to become reinforcing by itself.

Dogs have primary and secondary reinforcers, too. Creative dog trainers keep track of what is reinforcing for the dog they are working with, and the list can be rather different for each dog. There is a range of food reinforcers that dogs value, from low-level dry dog biscuits to high-

value steak tidbits and liverwurst. Among the favorites for many Chihuahuas are hot dogs, cheese bits, chicken and freeze dried liver. Dogs value soft, whole food, high protein treats over dry biscuits any time.

Which one you select can depend on how difficult the behavior was, how distracting the environment is, or how long you have been working on the task. If the behavior was more difficult, the dog made a leap in criteria, or performed the behavior in a high-stress or very distracting environment, you can up the stakes, pun intended, by giving a jackpot of extra high-value treats such as freeze dried liver or hot dogs.

Other reinforcers can include opportunities to engage in play such as activities like a game of tug, chasing a ball or other favored toy, or performing a favorite behavior like jumping to hit a hand target. This is the Premack Principle in action. For some Chihuahuas, the chance to engage in some play or activities can be even more reinforcing than food.

Secondary reinforcement for dogs include the use of marker signals such as clickers or whistles, or verbal markers such as "yes." What all of these have in common is that they were previously neutral, but with consistent pairing with primary reinforcement they been conditioned to become reinforcing. Sometimes secondary reinforcers such as a clicker are referred to as a "bridge" because it is such a strong signal that primary reinforcement is coming that it bridges the interval of time between the behavior marked and the presentation of primary reinforcement.

Clickers are excellent conditioned reinforcers and are sometimes referred to as an event marker, which gives you a clue as to the correct timing of their use. Their neutral sound stands out in the environment, they are quickly conditioned by pairing with high-value food, and they are an easy tool to put into use almost immediately. Clickers are also wonderful tools for beginner dog trainers, because if you make a mistake and wrongly time your click, or click the wrong behavior, you can immediately fix it, without the drawbacks of using punishers. Just simply adjust your timing, and click correctly on the next repetition. You get what you click!

Of course, you don't always have use of a clicker, so you can also condition a verbal marker, such as the word "yes". It's not quite as clear for your Chihuahua, but if you link it consistently to a primary reinforcer to condition it, and use it with the same timing during training as the actual clicker or other event marker, it will suffice as a stand-in. If the behavior degrades, you can always dig out your clicker and polish it up again.

Punishers: Are They Ever Appropriate?

A natural question if we are using rewards to increase certain behaviors, is shouldn't we also be using punishment to decrease other behaviors? The answer is maybe, depending on what kind of punishment you are referring to.

Like reinforcement, punishment is broken down into positive and negative punishment. While both kinds of punishment will have the end effect of decreasing the occurrence of a particular behavior, the difference between the application of the two kinds of punishers can be stark and potentially inhumane.

Positive punishment occurs with the addition of an unpleasant, sometimes highly aversive consequence, with the result that the behavior is less likely to be repeated. Commonly used punishers include verbal reprimands, collar corrections, slapping the dog under the chin, shock collars, and spraying water bottles. However, the consequence has to be applied with enough intensity and the correct timing to be effective without going overboard and becoming abusive, which is incredibly difficult to do.

Furthermore, while the positive punisher will suppress the undesired behavior if applied correctly, it does not tell the dog what the correct behavior is, so often there is spontaneous recovery after the punishment stops. Now, you have to start over.

Lastly, most species are able to adapt or habituate to punishers over time, so you have to keep increasing the intensity to make it effective. Because of all the difficulties in applying positive punishers correctly, they are almost useless as a training tool for the average pet owner.

Negative punishers, on the other hand, can be just as effective with the same result in decreasing unwanted behavior. Negative punishment involves removal of a potential positive consequence. In other words, withholding a reinforcer can be a punisher to a dog that was willing to work for that reward. Negative punishment can be easy to effectively deliver, especially if you've done your homework and know what your Chihuahua's reinforcers are.

For example, if your Chihuahua is jumping on and nipping guests for attention, the reinforcer that is keeping the jumping behavior going, coaching guests to ignore your Chihuahua until he has all four feet on the ground can be an effective negative punisher for the jumping and nipping. If done consistently, and then appropriate behavior such as sitting for greetings is reinforced with the petting, this is a much more humane way to decrease the jumping behavior than with positive punishers such as pinching the dog or shocking him for jumping up.

Another typical application of negative punishers is with mouthy puppies. If mouthing and gnawing is reaching an unacceptable intensity, stopping play and walking away from the puppy for a brief twenty second time-out can negatively punish the biting behavior. Again, if done immediately and consistently, you will see a decrease in the behavior you are trying to inhibit.

Aversives: A Slippery Slope!

Punishers, especially positive punishers, rely on a consequence that is unpleasant, or aversive, so that the dog will decrease the unwanted behavior. As we've learned, those consequences have to be aversive enough to stop the behavior without the dog habituating to it.

Do you ever see a dog getting leash jerks all the way down the street for pulling his frustrated owner? It is something that happens all the time. That dog has habituated to the collar correction, and unless the owner is willing to pull the dog right off his feet and choke him the next time the dog pulls on the leash, he is never going to decrease that behavior using that punisher. They will just continue the struggle, with the dog ignoring the punisher, and the owner hesitant to increase the punisher to an effective level, until leash walking is a miserable experience for both of them, and they stop going for walks. Everybody loses.

So when people have run out of punishers that work, they begin to increase the intensity or frequency of punishment in a never-ending battle to find the one that works, for now. They apply that collar harder, tighter, or more often, they switch from slip collar to prong collar, they switch from water squirts to shocking dogs. Do you see the pattern?

What they are also forgetting are the side effects that accompany applying aversive punishment. The dog is not stupid, and quickly picks up that the aversive comes from you, or only happens when you are present. Quickly, things can spiral into abusive practices, and result in both fear and aggression directed at whoever is applying the aversive punisher, or others in the environment. This last point can make applying aversive punishers very, very dangerous.

If you find that you have started to introduce punishment into your training practice and then have started down the slippery slope of increasing the aversives in an attempt to solve a behavior problem, you are probably in over your head. Find an experienced positive-reinforcement trainer to help you solve your training problem in a more humane way.

Capture Behaviors You Do Want

One of the more difficult mechanical skills to learn when using positive-reinforcement training techniques is to pick out behaviors you want to mark and reward. Easier said than done. Especially when you are trying to mark and reward specific behaviors; you will have to train your eye to pick them out to capture them with your clicker. As we know, timing your click well is critical to successful marking of behavior.

Most trainers will have you practice and improve those mechanical skills in a variety of ways, using some exercises without your Chihuahua. Some of them require a partner, some of them a prop such as a ball, and there are a variety of online resources for exploring learning-theory concepts, the most famous of which is Sniffy, The Virtual Rat.

An easy exercise to try is to click a bouncing ball. You can bounce a ball, and click every time the ball hits the ground. This is a simple but effective technique, since you can hear if your clicks are mistimed. A slightly more difficult exercise is to toss the ball in the air and click when it reaches the highest point before it comes back down.

The online games can be challenging, but fun. My personal favorite is one that you have to click sheep that try to run out of the herd. If you're too slow, they get away. If you click too fast because a sheep looks at you, but then doesn't move, you get a penalty.

A popular and comprehensive practice model available online is Sniffy, the Virtual Rat, developed by faculty at the University of Toronto at Mississauga. Sniffy is a simulation of a rat in a Skinner Box developed for teaching operant conditioning principles to psychology and animal behavior students. You can learn about reinforcement and punishment, in-depth, by training Sniffy to fear a sound or light or to press a bar to obtain food, without having to invest in the purchase of an actual rat. Then you progress to studies of more

complex learning phenomena and, of course, can teach Sniffy tricks.

Certainly, the easiest way to hone observation skills is to watch a dog. Sit somewhere you can observe your Chihuahua from a distance with paper and pencil, like a backyard or the dog park. Decide to track one behavior your Chihuahua does regularly, say, sniffing. Watch your Chihuahua for a set duration, maybe ten minutes, and make a mark every time your Chihuahua repeats the behavior. Then pick another behavior, say tail wagging, to track for the next ten minutes. As you watch your Chihuahua engage in different activities, you will be training yourself to pick out particular behaviors. Even experi-

enced dog trainers can benefit from practicing these observation skills.

Don't Reinforce Behaviors You Don't Want

While you're capturing behaviors you want to mark with your clicker, you also have to be very careful you're not accidentally reinforcing other behaviors you would rather not see repeated. Remember, reinforcement is any consequence that increases the occurrence of the behavior directly before it. Start to pay close attention; if your Chihuahua is repeating a behavior consistently, try to pick out what occurs immediately after that that may be reinforcing the behavior.

Reinforcement is the primary way that all of those annoying behaviors—like jumping on guests for attention, nuisance barking, barking or whining for attention, snatching laundry, and food stealing or begging at the table, among others are maintained. Often, the reinforcement is coming from somewhere else in the environment, say, your neighbor that allows your Chihuahua to jump on him for greetings or your husband that gives the begging dog a tidbit off his plate when you're not looking.

One of the hallmarks of an effective trainer is being able to see how behaviors are being reinforced by other people or the environment and then setting it up so that the reinforcement stops. Once the reinforcement stops, the behavior will

change, too. Of course, that's not always as easy as it sounds.

For example, many people are at a loss when their Chihuahua has taken to whining and barking at them for attention when they sit down to read the newspaper or a book. The first few times it happens, most people give Fido a halfhearted pet or two to "soothe" him, hoping Fido will wander off now that he's gotten what he wanted. Wrong! Fido has now been reinforced with attention, for the behavior of whining and barking at his companion. Guess what behavior is now going to occur more frequently?

After the next few occurrences, Fido's owner gets a bit annoyed. "Go away, I'm busy!" he scolds, while trying to finish reading his newspaper. Guess what? Verbal reinforcement! Fido still got some attention, so the behavior continues, and starts to get stronger.

Quickly this scenario turns into a battle. Fido whines, barks, and otherwise demands attention now, and his exasperated owner begins to think about devising punishers to "stop" the behavior, when in all actuality, it never would have started if his owner had not accidentally reinforced it the very first time it happened. By simply getting up and walking away from Fido when he let loose with the torrent of demands for attention, the owner would have extinguished it immediately.

Often, it's difficult to really control all the reinforcement that drives your Chihuahua's behavior. What becomes more important is that when you do recognize when reinforcement is actually maintaining a behavior you don't want, you rectify it by reinforcing another, more appropri-

ate behavior. If you consistently reinforce incompatible behavior, you can in effect change the behavior before it has a chance to be reinforced.

In the example above, when Fido's exasperated companion recognized a pattern of demanding attention by whining or barking when he sat down to read the newspaper, he had a choice. Ignoring the behavior, hoping for extinction may work, but the dog may try another, even more inappropriate behavior like nipping.

Alternately, and ultimately more effective in the long run, he could see Fido coming and cue a behavior such as "settle," essentially a relaxed stay in the down position. Now he should actively reinforce Fido for relaxing by petting, giving him an activity to keep him busy, or even clicking and treating him, slowly building up the time Fido can settle quietly.

Using Behavior Markers

Behavior markers are conditioned reinforcers used to signal that the behavior marked will earn reinforcement. In other words, "That was correct, and here comes the treat."

Dog trainers typically use a sound, word, signal, or metal clicker to mark the exact moment a dog is correct. For example, the moment the dog's bottom hits the floor in a sit, a trainer would use his marker to tell the dog that was the right behavior. That marker would immediately be followed by reinforcement, often food but whatever else the dog values is fine, increasing the probability that the behavior will be repeated.

Clicker Training?

Clicker training refers to training using operant conditioning principles, using a behavior marker linked to positive reinforcement of high value. Clicker trainers routinely leave out negative reinforcement and positive punishment, due to the unwanted side effects of inhibiting behavior and forming negative associations with the trainer.

Of course, not all behavior makers are created equal. Marking the behavior with a novel sound (CLICK!) helps the dog process precise information quickly and speeds up the training process immensely. Other behavior markers can be used, such as a verbal "yes!", a flashlight or thumbs-up motion for a deaf dog, or a whistle, but a clicker is distinctive and loud enough to stand out.

Using a distinctive sound, such as a click, allows us to mark exactly which behavior earned the reward. That's why clicker trainers call the click an "event marker" or "bridging signal." The click bridges or connects the behavioral event and its reward.

Ten Easy Tips for Clicker Training Your Chihuahua

1. Pick a behavior to get started with. Begin with something your Chihuahua already does but that you haven't really gotten under control yet, such as sitting in front of you or lying down when you sit on the couch.

2. Click once just as your Chihuahua does the behavior, then follow up with a tiny, high-value treat.

3. Click once. If you want to increase the value of the reinforcement for a particularly good response, give two or more tiny treats.

4. The click ends the behavior, so don't be alarmed if your Chihuahua pops out of position when he hears the click. Just deliver the treat and move on to the next rep.

5. If you want to increase the duration of the behavior, slightly delay the click for a few seconds at a time.

6. Keep sessions short. More is learned in ten good repetitions than twenty-five poor repetitions.

7. Don't wait for a finished behavior to click. Instead click for approximations, or small segments of the total behavior.

If you are teaching down, you can click your Chihuahua moving toward the ground, and then click his chest touching the ground, and then his whole body touching the ground. Every discrete behavior has approximations.

8. Carefully increase your criteria. When teaching your Chihuahua to sit, don't increase the duration of the behavior to ten seconds, if he is not confident for five seconds.

9. Use clicking for teaching incompatible behaviors. Click your Chihuahua for sitting for greetings instead of jumping to say hello. Click your Chihuahua for settling quietly on a mat when you eat your meals, rather than table begging.

10. When your Chihuahua is offering the behavior to get you to click, label it with the cue. Begin to click only when you've given the cue, and ignore the behavior when a cue wasn't given.

Do You Have to Use a Clicker?

Using a standout sound like a metal clicker is an important piece of the program. The sound or signal has to be clear and concise and not something your Chihuahua will hear in other contexts, to avoid confusion.

Of course, trainers have a variety of markers that fit those criteria. Although dog trainers typically use metal clickers to mark behavior, dolphin and whale trainers often make use of whistles. Researchers training lab animals often use a buzz, tone, or flashing light to mark behaviors.

In a pinch, dog trainers have used bottle caps, pens, and their mouths to make a pop or cluck sound to mark behavior, as well as single, distinctive spoken word such as "Yes." Trainers working with deaf dogs use a thumbs-up signal, a flash of a penlight, or the vibration on an electronic collar to mark behavior.

Any distinctive sound or signal you can provide consistently can be linked to reinforcement and used as a behavior marker. However, that doesn't mean any old thing will work.

For example, it's very unlikely that a sound the handler makes vocally will be consistent enough to condition well for use with a novice dog learning new behaviors. However, many trainers are adept at delivering a marker word such as "Yes!" in a neutral, consistent manner when working with more experienced dogs.

Other markers, such as clicking sounds from pens or bottle caps that sound fine up close, often don't carry the distance when you start moving away from your Chihuahua. They are lost in the wind or the sound of passing traffic or barking dogs.

So, although many dog trainers experiment a bit with finding a good marker system, they often rely on the old standby, a metal clicker, to fulfill their needs for marking new behaviors, especially when training inexperienced dogs. It's clear, concise, and conditions quickly.

Linking Your Marker to a Reinforcer

It sounds simple, just click and follow up with a treat. So, how does your Chihuahua make the connection between that sound, the behavior, and the reward?

If your Chihuahua is startled by the clicking sound initially, or won't eat after hearing the sound, you should modify the sound. Hold the clicker behind your back, hold it in your pocket, or wrap it in tape to muffle the sound initially. It is loud, and some dogs are easily startled especially if you are directing the sound toward them. If the dog still won't eat, try a softer sound such as a pen cap click. Once your Chihuahua is comfortable with the softer sound, you can reintroduce the muffled clicker, and then move onto using it at full volume.

Jump-Start Your Behaviors: Luring and Shaping

There are various ways to get a behavior to occur, but not all are created equal. The primary tools positive-reinforcement trainers use are luring and shaping to get a behavior to happen so that they can mark and reinforce it.

To lure or not to lure is a question many trainers debate. Luring is a technique in which the trainer leads the dog though the behavior with a valued treat or toy and then delivers the reinforcer at the moment the dog attains success. The trainer is working in proximity with the dog and can deliver reinforcement with the appropriate timing, so marking isn't really necessary. Think of it as an extra hint for a novice dog, since you are sort of helping him find the behavior, rather than relying on him to figure it out for himself.

Conditioning the clicker correctly does follow the basic principle of classical conditioning. If your Chihuahua hears a click, and that is immediately followed by the food, the click becomes a predictor that the food is coming.

Charge up, or link, the sound and food by clicking and immediately giving your Chihuahua a tiny, high value treat. Do this ten or fifteen times in a row, just click-treat, click-treat, click-treat. After the series, click once and observe your Chihuahua's response. He should look expectantly for a treat. Now you know the conditioning is established.

If you present the food before he hears the click, the click will not be relevant to your Chihuahua. It's just extraneous noise that happens during a training session, so be careful with your timing. If your timing is correct and your food delivery is fluent, go ahead and start training.

It's so easy to lure a pup into a sit by holding a treat in front of his nose and then using it to bring his head up and his hind end down into a sit. Bingo, deliver your treat. Another easy lure may be to clap your hands, hold up a toy and back away from a puppy to lure a recall. Over a few repetitions, you could quickly fade out the lure while adding a cue and still retain the recall behavior if you have reinforced it for the puppy.

There are, however, some drawbacks to relying too heavily on this method. Often, the handler relies on the lure long after it is needed. If the handler does not quickly fade use of the lure, the dog will need the lure to do the behavior. In fact, it may become the cue: see and follow hand, butt on floor, reward. It may be confusing for the dog and frustrating for the novice handler to try to switch to a verbal cue if he or she has stayed at this stage for too long.

That's not to say that you should never use luring as a way to elicit a behavior. Instead, if you find you need to lure a behavior to jump-start it quickly, or your Chihuahua is not yet comfortable offering behavior to shape, you should use the smallest possible lure and use it the least amount of times. Start fading the lure as soon as the behavior is readily performed using the lure.

For example, if you are teaching your Chihuahua to spin in a circle, lure with your whole flat hand a few times, clicking and treating for success. Once the dog gets "follow the hand in a circle" successfully, fade the hand to just a finger. On the next few repetitions, lure with a pointed finger, and begin to make the circles smaller.

At this stage, begin to offer the signal a bit earlier, turning the signal into a cue, rather than a lure. Then you can fade it further until your motion is a tiny fingertip circle with your hand held at your waist. There, you've gotten rid of that pesky lure, or more accurately, turned it into a subtle hand signal.

Shaping is another, sometimes more elegant way to get to a behavior. Instead of helping the dog attain a behavior with the lure, you would let the dog offer approximations of it on his own to get reinforcement. Many trainers prefer this method, thinking it encourages the problem solving and independent thinking required in a dog going on to advanced training.

When shaping a behavior from scratch, the trainer selects a series of approximations to reinforce, building on each level once the dog has mastered it. Sometimes, however, this process is difficult or frustrating for a novice dog and beginner trainer, and if the trainer can't select a behavior to click, the training will stop before it even gets started.

Using the previous example of teaching your Chihuahua to spin, you would select a first approximation to click, such as your Chihuahua glancing to the left side. Once the dog is looking left for the click, you would select a full head turn, then perhaps leaning to the left, or foot movement left, then partially around a circle, then turning all the way around.

Shaping is a great way to sharpen your skills at selecting approximations of behavior. Once you and your Chihuahua are comfortable with the clicker rules, and your Chihuahua is happy to offer new things for you to click, go ahead and begin shaping some simple behaviors. Don't be intimidated. Shaping is considered the "gold standard" in training complex, fluent behavior, and results in a Chihuahua being able to learn quickly and problem solve—as well as being incredibly fun!

Many trainers will use a combination of luring and shaping to train a behavior. Jump-starting it using a lure and then finishing and fine-tuning a behavior using shaping is a both efficient and user friendly. After all, your goal is to get the final behavior so you can reinforce it quickly, so use both tools to get you there.

Ready Rules of Reinforcement

Two difficult concepts for beginning trainers to become comfortable with are criteria selection, or selecting which behaviors to click, and schedules of reinforcement, or how frequently to click and when to stop clicking a behavior. Let's start with how to select behavior, or even segments of a behavior called approximations, to click.

Criteria Selection: The Whole Thing or Just a Piece?

We've explored how important it is to reinforce behaviors a dog offers. It seems relatively straightforward: you see something you like, maybe a sit or down, click it and it will happen again.

But sometimes the finished behavior is rather complex, and has a variety of components to master. Take for example sitting in heel position. Chances are, your Chihuahua isn't going to just offer it in finished, perfect form.

Initially, you might have to select approximations of the sit behavior by shaping or luring the dog's head up and clicking as his rump goes down. You will have to train your eye to capture approximations of a behavior with your clicker, timing your click well to successfully mark that piece of the behavior.

Begin by standing in front of the dog and getting his attention. When he looks up at your face, it's very likely he will lean backwards to lift his head and make eye contact. Click and treat the leaning backwards, that may be your first approximation. On the next repetition, he may lean further backwards, so click and treat that one, too.

After a few repetitions of this, he should lean further until he has to bend his back legs, and dip his back end toward the ground to maintain eye contact. This might get a jackpot! Now, your next approximation should be clicking the bending of the back legs, and just ignore any repetitions that don't include this approximation.

In this way you will shape the behavior, until your Chihuahua is attentively sitting on the floor. Now you can start to select additional criteria to add to the exercise, such as how quickly he sits, what direction he is facing when he sits, where he sits in relation to the handler, and for how long he sits.

Criterion selection should be simple to ensure the dog's success, and build on the previous criterion. Initially, you may be clicking every time your Chihuahua meets the initial criterion of "butt on ground." It doesn't matter if he immediately pops up or is facing the wrong direction or anything else. After all, your only criterion was "butt on ground."

Once your Chihuahua is offering the "butt on ground" behavior reliably, with at least 80-percent accuracy, select your next criterion for the behavior, say "hold butt on ground for three seconds." You would click every time your Chihuahua sits for three seconds, not less. Once the dog can sit for three seconds, your next criterion might be five seconds, working toward several minutes in position at a time.

Other criteria you select might include are how quickly your Chihuahua sits (immediately is good), how far away from you your Chihuahua is (right next to you), what side he is on and what direction he is facing (on your left side, facing forward). You keep building toward your final goal of the sit-stay in-heel position, one criterion at a time.

Breaking Down Behaviors for Success: Lumping versus Splitting

The most difficult task in training can be criteria selection, and by the far the most common mistake dog trainers make is lumping too many criterion together and frustrating or confusing the dog.

Teachers of humans are adept at recognizing criteria selection in their pupils.

For example, when teaching a first grader to read individual words (one level of criteria in fluent reading skills), the teacher would not next expect that the child could read a college textbook. It would require about twelve years of practice, increasing through many levels of criteria, before the child reaches that level of fluency in the behavior of stringing letters into words, and words into sentences, and sentences into paragraphs with meaning.

Following the same example, the level of criteria of reading the words at the first-grade level could be broken down even further. Teaching the child to recognize the individual letters, and then the sounds they each make, is shaping the behavior of reading words, which could then be shaped into reading that textbook at the higher level.

Criteria selection for Chihuahuas follows the same premise. If you move too quickly, lumping the criteria, the dog will be overwhelmed quickly and the behavior will fall apart. Of course, if you move too slowly and stay too long at one level, your Chihuahua will stop moving up the shaping ladder to the finished behavior.

Generally, you should not move up the ladder until your Chihuahua has attained 80 percent or better correct responses in a session, that is eight out of ten repetitions at that level of criteria in a session are correct.

If your Chihuahua is making more than one or two errors in a session, stop and rethink your criteria selection. You have probably lumped multiple criteria and will need to break it down smaller to avoid frustrating your Chihuahua and setting him up to fail.

Adding a Cue to Get It Under Control

So far, we've talked about how to get the party started with luring or shaping, and how to select criteria to click, but we really haven't talked about what to call these behaviors. We haven't, even once, told your Chihuahua to do the behavior. Clicker trainers usually save this part until after something resembling the final behavior is established.

Initially, the cue word is really just chatter in the room, another bit of extraneous information the dog has to block out while he is concentrating on learning something new. Dogs don't speak English, so verbal chatter, cheerleading, and slinging commands at the dog before an association is made with a behavior is pointless. Make learning easier by keeping noise to a minimum, and let the clicker tell the dog what's right.

Once your Chihuahua is offering the almost finished behavior at least 80 percent of the time, it is time to give that behavior a name. However, before you can use the cue to elicit the behavior, you have to associate the word, or hand signal, with the finished behavior and make it stick.

Begin conditioning the cue by saying it, or showing a hand signal, as the dog does the behavior. Your Chihuahua will move into position, say the cue or give the hand signal, then click and treat. Repeat this thirty times or more, making sure you are giving the cue in the same manner each time.

You must also be sure nothing else in the environment is consistent, because the dog may condition to something other than what you intend. Move your body in a natural carriage, changing position frequently, varying the distance and position relative to the dog, and make sure you relax your eye contact and body tension as you label the repetitions with the cue word. Many Chihuahuas think "Sit" means "hold butt on ground while the human stands still with her hands at her sides, staring at me, and holding her breath." Oops. You want the dog to think "Sit" means "hold butt on ground, no matter what the human is doing."

Keep in mind your Chihuahua may respond better to hand signals than verbal cues. Dogs are visually aware, as most of their language is subtle body signals.

They don't have verbal language, so our constant stream of chitchat is largely irrelevant to them. They just don't have the ear for language, except for those words that have a direct association for them ("cookie," "walk," "car," and "sit" are the words most Chihuahuas know). Introducing hand signals for common behaviors early can clear up your communication.

Once your Chihuahua has heard the cue word while he does a behavior a number of times, he will link that word with the behavior, and associate the cue and behavior with the coming reinforcement. Begin to say the cue, or give your hand signal, a bit earlier now, just as the dog is almost into position. For the sit, for example, you would give your signal as the dog was halfway to the ground, and then click and treat when the dog is all the way

down. Repeat this for another set of repetitions.

For the third stage, you will back up the cue to the beginning of the behavior. As your Chihuahua is standing, give your cue to sit as he just begins to move into position, maybe when he begins leaning backward to bend his legs (remember your earliest approximation). He should follow through to get the click.

Finally, you can set up the behavior just as above and say your verbal cue, expecting the dog to move into position to get his click. Now it's a conditioned cue. Jackpot your Chihuahua!

Now that you have a cue that elicits the behavior, you can stop reinforcing uncued repetitions of the behavior. If he gets clicked every time he offers a sit, he will just keep guessing that you might want him to sit, and it might pay off. It will never be under stimulus control. Later, we will learn how to proof, or generalize, the behavior so he can do it everywhere!

Schedules of Reinforcement: When to Stop Clicking

A common question, besides what criteria to click, is how often and when you should stop clicking. You can't always walk around with a clicker and treats, can you? How do we get from clicking approximations of a behavior, to clicking as we shape it into a finished behavior, to clicking a chain of more than one behavior, to main-

taining the behavior for the long term without clicking at all? Understanding schedules of reinforcement becomes critical to your success.

There is both a science and an art to understanding rules of reinforcement, and they are always in play, whether you are teaching something new or maintaining something old. The truth is, although there are general rules regarding reinforcement rates, they can change depending on the behavior you're teaching, what stage you're working on, and the dog you're working with.

Let's look at a typical progression for training your Chihuahua to enter his crate on cue. Most trainers would agree that initially you should mark every approximation of the behavior for the dog, even if it's not in finished form. In this case, maybe just looking at the crate or

approaching it will earn the dog a click. This stage may go slowly for a timid Chihuahua, using the clicker to mark individual steps over several sessions, or it may proceed very quickly for a confident dog that knows the "clicker game" and is jumping into the crate within three clicks.

As you go up the shaping ladder you would continue to click every repetition at each increased level of criteria (look at crate, move toward crate, touch crate, front legs in, back legs in, whole body in and turn around, close door, etc.), while dropping out clicking for the level below. For example, if your Chihuahua is offering to enter the crate reliably, don't continue to click him for just looking at it.

Many trainers would also agree that once you have a discrete behavior that is almost in final form, such as getting into the crate and settling down on the mat, you should continue to mark the behavior each time until it is on cue, or under stimulus control. Clicking and treating every time the dog does the behavior successfully is referred to as a continuous reinforcement schedule.

Of course, your end goal is to elicit the behavior on cue many times, without having to use a clicker and treats every time. You will have to drop down the rate of reinforcement to maintenance levels, then switch to a "real-life" reinforcer that you can deliver at that rate. In general, you will start to move away from training scenarios with continuous reinforcement (reinforcing every time) and switch to an intermittent schedule (reinforcing some of the time) with real-life reinforcers like fun stuff, toys, access to attention or resources, doing a new behavior, or whatever your Chihuahua loves in life.

So, how do you know when to start changing the schedule? If your pup is fluent in the new behavior, meaning he can attain the behavior on cue at least 90 percent of the time, and you are done adding additional criteria for the dog to meet, you can start to switch to an intermittent reinforcement schedule. This is the first step in stopping clicking altogether.

Begin with dropping out the clicker for one out of ten repetitions, then perhaps

two or three out of ten, and so on. Which repetitions you don't click should be random, but you should still be selecting for the better ones. Continue dropping out clicks until your Chihuahua can do at least ten repetitions in a row, not knowing which one of them you're going to click and treat. This random intermittent schedule will make behavior stronger and maintain it for as long as you continue to intermittently reinforce it.

At this stage you should also begin to add different types of reinforcement to the mix, Sometimes you will click and treat. Sometimes you will say "Yes!" and introduce a tug toy, throw a ball or offer an opportunity to perform another wonderful behavior (a dog's favorite might be to reward the sit with a leap into your lap). Use any other wonderfully exciting reinforcer other than food.

Your goal is to maintain the behavior using real-life reinforcers and wean off the click and treat altogether for the finished behavior. Think of it as your Chihuahua playing a slot machine—oh, the excitement! He doesn't know which repetition will pay off, but one of these is gonna be good, and he can't wait to find out which one! This reinforcement schedule will keep the behavior going for long stretches of time. Keep your reinforcers interesting and surprising, and your Chihuahua will work like a dog!

Try to remember that behavior, even very well-trained and very discreet behavior, is always changing. If you train your Chihuahua to spin in a circle and then five days later stop reinforcing it completely, the behavior will go away (extinction). If your training is sloppy and you give your Chihuahua a click and a treat for a slow or incomplete spin, the behavior will degrade, and you will get more slow or incomplete spins. So you must get the spinning behavior to the level of criteria that you require (spinning quickly, all the way around, and in the same direction each time) and then maintain it for the long term with the right rate (intermittent) and kinds of reinforcement (real life).

Where in the World Is Fido? Generalizing Behavior

Once you have shaped a fluent behavior, it's strongly on cue, you're done, right? Not so fast. You still have to help your Chihuahua learn to perform the behavior in a variety of locations with different distractions. You need generalize the behavior.

Dogs are masters at making associations. Often, dog owners can't even say "cookie," "car," or "cat" without getting a big reaction. These words are not directly taught to dogs. They made the association on their own, quickly.

Although dogs make associations quickly, such as "that hand motion means put my butt on the ground, and I'll get a treat," they are poor at generalizing that knowledge to other situations. For example, often you can tell which room an owner has trained a new behavior in based on the dog's response in different locations. It is usually strongest in the kitchen (after all, that's where the treats

are), weaker in the living room, and completely absent in the bathroom. No one trains anything in the bathroom, so the dog has no reinforcement history for sitting in the bathroom. In other words, the rules of sit may not apply here.

One way to help a Chihuahua make the leap is to design your training sessions to resemble real life quickly. You would not ask your Chihuahua to sit only when in the kitchen, so why would you only train in the kitchen?

I ask students to play a little game called "Where in the World is Fido?" with each new behavior to help their dog generalize his new skill. I know when I ask "Where?" that an answer of "Fido is sitting in the living room on cue" is not as well generalized as "Fido is sitting at the park on cue in the presence of moving ducks."

Every practice session should include criteria change regarding the location of training, and this exercise can be done while you are still on a continuous reinforcement schedule. For example, one day practice in the living room, mastering facing all four directions and assuming as many orientations as you can think of in that room, clicking and treating all successful repetitions. Sometimes you are facing your Chihuahua, sometimes you are facing away from your Chihuahua. Sometimes you are standing up, sometimes you are sitting in a chair. Sometimes you are in a yoga position, sometimes you are facing the wall.

Continue to move each training session around the house until you have mastered the skill in every conceivable indoor location that you can think of, including the bathroom, using every possible orientation you can think of in that location (try lying in the tub).

Then, move outdoors! Starting in the quietest location you can think of. Maybe start practice sitting in the backyard, and then move it to the front yard; practice in the neighbor's driveway; take a short walk down the block to practice; then take a drive to the park. Practice in front of the local supermarket, inside a pet store, on the front steps of your local library, and so on.

When you play "Where in the World Is Fido?" you are honing your dog's skills and getting the behavior under stimulus control independent of visual, noise, and

other distractions; indoor and outdoor settings; and in all weather conditions to generalize the behavior. Don't short-change the work you've done to get the behavior trained by failing to generalize it to every location! Eventually your Chihuahua will get it, and you will have a reliable skill to use anywhere.

Why Do I Feel Like An Octopus?

When you first try clicker training, you may feel like you need eight arms with treats, clickers, tug toys, tennis balls, a leash attached to a jumping dog, a bait bag, and poop bags in your pocket. Where do you put everything? You may feel like you are never going to be coordinated enough to get this under control! By thinking ahead, and with a little experience, you will soon be fluent in your behavior, too.

Managing Your Training to Make It Flow

First things first. Give yourself room to work, preferably a contained area, with minimal distractions for both you and your Chihuahua. Now you can get rid of your leash, or at least just let the dog trail it around, or you could just step on it, or tie it to your belt to keep your Chihuahua from wandering off. In other words, you really don't need it in your hand, because you won't be using it for "corrections."

Second, you will need one hand for your clicker. Your food does not need to be in your hand, or even on your body. In fact, it's even better if it's not! If you're luring a behavior, however, one piece in your hand should suffice. Good, now you're not dropping free treats all over the place, distracting the dog.

What are your Chihuahua's top three reinforcers? Have those close by, say, in a pocket, bait bag, or on the counter. You should not be waving treats or tennis balls in the dog's face as he works. It's a distraction, as well as no longer a reinforcement; if the treats are there before the behavior, it's bribery.

Remember, the clicker is a bridging stimulus and buys you a little time for the presentation of the reinforcer. So you do have time to click and reach for the treat on the counter; it does not have to be in your hand. You should not be reaching for anything until after the click.

So, if you have the leash off or under control, a clicker in one hand, and reinforcement nearby, and perhaps one tidbit in your other hand to use as a lure, you are ready to train without eight arms. You can now concentrate on your clear timing of the click and quick presentation of the reinforcement.

Your fluency with clicker training will improve over time, and then you will not even think about all these other things. You will just train and have a great time doing it. Of course, if you are working outdoors, keep that poop bag handy. You should give your pup an opportunity to potty before training begins, but Mother Nature calls at inopportune times.

Keeping Track of Your Progress

Once you are training, you need to develop a tracking system to keep your sessions organized. Keeping some sort of record will help you organize what you want to accomplish in a session, record how your Chihuahua has performed, plan your next session, and note what has not been successful.

You will need to track all kinds of information, including but not limited to:
- which behavior you are working on right now
- what level of criteria are you working at
- how many reps you have done
- how many have been successful
- what is your next level of criteria
- how you can break this level down to smaller criteria if your dog is not attaining success
- what your reinforcement rate is and whether it is continuous or intermittent
- what your reinforcers for each session are, and whether you can insert any real-life reinforcers
- whether you are ready to generalize this behavior

Keeping all of your data organized becomes critical once you are training more than one behavior or more than one Chihuahua! While you may be working on generalizing the sit, you may still be luring or shaping a more elaborate behavior. Each behavior you're working on may be at separate stages of criteria, and you will quickly lose track if it's all in your head.

10 *Five Top Skills to Teach Your Chihuahua*

Foundation Skills for Every Chihuahua

It can be difficult to narrow down what your Chihuahua really needs to know, and overwhelming to know where to start. There are dozens of potential skills and tricks you could teach, but how do you know what you should start with, and what is really necessary?

It is a good idea to start training for all new puppies with some general skills that can be used whether they are expected to be house pets, show dogs, therapy or service dogs, or even to excel at competitive dog sports. Recently adopted adult dogs coming into the home will also benefit from a quick review of the basics as a way to help them learn the ropes in the new environment.

Every puppy, and every newly adopted adult Chihuahua, should have some basic skills that will help you direct their behavior and keep them safe. These skills should include conditioned attention, sit, down, stay, controlled leash walking with polite greetings of dogs and people, and a solid recall in any location. These are the foundation skills that will give you a polite, well-rounded dog and that can be easily developed into more advanced skills. So, whatever age your Chihuahua is, let's get started.

It All Starts with Attention

Most trainers start with the very same foundation skill, namely, conditioned attention. Sounds strange, right? After all, your Chihuahua knows his name, why can't you just use that to get his attention? Not so fast. While most dogs quickly condition that their name means "look at the human saying my name, something good might happen," it just as often means "stop what you're doing," "come over here," "you're cute," "we're going in the car," "time for dinner," and "let me pet you."

You will say your Chihuahua's name dozens of times a day, and much of the time it will not be followed by anything really relevant to your dog. Often, dogs learn to just ignore humans unless something else is in the picture. When you say your Chihuahua's name while you are holding food, a leash, or a toy, it suddenly becomes relevant. So, how can you circumvent this phenomenon and condition the dog to pay attention every time you ask for it? You can use something other than his name.

Teaching an attention cue also has a wonderful side effect: It teaches the dog to check in with you more frequently and pay attention to you in all sorts of environments. Your Chihuahua will learn to listen for the next cue, which may be "Sit," or "Down," or "Come." If your Chihuahua is looking at you and then doing one of those behaviors, he can't be barking at people on the street, pulling on his leash, or chasing cats or cars.

One way to teach attention is to reward eye contact, and then put it on cue. Start by holding a treat or small toy in your closed hand out to the side. Let your Chihuahua sniff, lick, and paw at your hand. He will try all kinds of behavior, even including barking at you. Eventually, he will look at you and maybe back up or sit down. Click when he backs away from your hand and makes eye contact, and then drop the treat on the floor. Repeat several times, moving around the room and assuming different positions, including standing, kneeling, and sitting on the floor. Your only consistent criteria should be that the dog makes eye contact.

If your Chihuahua seems excessively frustrated or confused the first time you practice attention, you can bring the treat hand up to your face a few times and then click as he makes eye contact while you hold the treat next to your cheek. Then, slowly start to hold your hand further and further from your body, until you can hold your arm straight out to the side and the dog immediately looks at your face.

Once your Chihuahua makes instant eye contact when you hold a treat or toy in your outstretched hand, you can add a verbal cue. Say "Fido, Look!" just as the dog makes eye contact, and then click and treat. With each session you practice, start to increase and vary the amount of time your Chihuahua must hold your gaze until you click and treat. For example, you might hold the position three seconds, five seconds, fifteen seconds, ten seconds, eight seconds, twenty seconds, ten seconds, and five seconds. Begin to increase the duration the dog must hold your gaze with every practice session, until when you say "Fido, Look" he will watch you for several minutes at a time while you move around the room.

This behavior will only be useful if you generalize it to other locations and contexts. Start to practice this in every location you can, and begin to request attention at times you are not in a training session. In distracting locations, you can warm up your Chihuahua with a few obvious repetitions, holding out your hand with the treat, then ask again after you put your hands down and he is looking at something or someone else. Jackpot these first few "cold trials," as you have added a big change in criteria and that's not easy for most dogs.

Mix in conditioned attention to real life, where the real learning takes place.

Go outside for a play session and mix a few "Fido, Look" repetitions into the game, throwing the toy as the reward. Before you feed your dog dinner or present an enrichment toy, ask for "Fido, Look." When you go to the park for a walk, get out of the car and immediately ask for a "Fido, Look" and use playtime as a reward for paying attention immediately. Now your Chihuahua is applying this skill to the real world, and now conditioned attention is not just a training game.

Sit and Stay

So, now that your Chihuahua is paying attention, let's deliver some real information. The quickest behavior to get under control is a sit. With a good sit comes a solid stay. After all, what good is it if your Chihuahua hits the floor like a champ, but can't hold it long enough for it to be a useful skill?

Puppies as young as six weeks, as well as adult dogs of any age, can attain this baseline behavior within days. It quickly

becomes a great way to direct your new Chihuahua's behavior to appropriate solutions for a long list of bad manners. If your Chihuahua is sitting when new friends approach, he can't jump. If he is sitting and paying attention to you while someone passes on the street, he is less likely to bark like a banshee, or chase dogs or kids on bikes and scooters. You have given him something else to do, and dogs don't really multi-task. If he is sitting on his

97

mat during mealtime, he cannot rudely solicit tidbits from your guests at the dinner table.

As you start to condition your Chihuahua to sit on cue, remember the basics of operant conditioning from Chapter 8. If you get the behavior, mark the behavior, and reward the behavior, the dog will repeat the behavior. Once he is repeating the behavior you can teach him to only offer it on cue, something called stimulus control, and then use the sit in all those situations you need your Chihuahua to be calm, settled, attentive, and out of trouble!

You can start your new Chihuahua sitting with a variety of methods. One of the easiest ways, though, is to lure the dog into a sit and capture it with your clicker! Start by holding your food lure, usually a tiny tidbit of chicken or cheese about the size of a raisin, directly in front of your Chihuahua's eyes and move it slowly and steadily toward the back of the pup's head. Your hand position is important, since holding it too high will cause your Chihuahua to jump, and moving it too fast will cause him to just back up. As your Chihuahua lifts his nose to follow the lure,

his weight will transfer to his hind legs, and he will sink back into the sit position. Keep your hand still until your Chihuahua sits, and then mark the behavior with a click and give your treat!

When your Chihuahua hears that click he will jump up. Don't worry—holding the position for any length of time comes later. Now he's in position to do another repetition of sit, so lure him right back into sit position again, click, and treat.

Do not tell the dog to sit or stay at this time; giving him too much verbal chit-chat can distract him. Be patient, and let him figure out that following his nose up, and folding his back end down, is what results in the reinforcement.

After the first five to ten reps your pup should start to offer the sit for you, sometimes called "recycling" the behavior. Now, your Chihuahua clearly understands what is getting reinforced and is purposefully offering it to get you to click! Once the puppy is recycling the behavior, you can start to make your hand motion smaller and begin to use an empty hand to signal the sit motion. You don't want to condition the dog that you must be holding a food lure over his head for him to sit.

An alternate method to teach the sit position is to shape the sit by waiting for your Chihuahua to do it on his own. Hang out in the same room as the dog, but just ignore him as you read the mail or check your e-mail, keeping one eye on your Chihuahua. He will get bored and eventually sit. Capture this behavior by immediately clicking and then throw him the treat.

Your Chihuahua will immediately jump up and get excited that you're playing a game, but you can just go back to ignor-

ing him again. When he gets bored again, he will sit. Capture this one, too. Within a few minutes the dog will be recycling the sits, trying to make you click. This is method is called free shaping a behavior, and will leave you one less step to fade out, namely, hand luring, before you move forward to true stimulus control.

Whatever method you use, after a few sessions of capturing the behavior with the clicker the puppy should be confidently offering a working version of the sit. Now is the time to assign it a verbal or hand cue that you can use to signal that he should sit to get the reinforcement. Once your Chihuahua offers the behavior only on cue, you will have true stimulus control.

The most straightforward way to help the dog get to this stage is to label the recycled behavior he is offering. Say the cue word or show a hand signal, a slow upward motion of the hand with your elbow held a waist level, just as the pup has moved into sit position. You should time the cue just as he does the behavior, wait a second or two and then click and treat.

You will label the behavior for your Chihuahua for several sets of repetitions, usually at least thirty times. For the next set begin to say or show the cue to the dog a millisecond before he moves into position. When training the sit, this would be after his back end starts to sit back, but before his rump hits the ground. Then slowly back up the cue until the cue is coming one second in front of the behavior.

By now, you should have established a cue that elicits the behavior. Once you have established this conditioned cue, and

it elicits the behavior consistently at least 90 percent of the time, you will stop reinforcing the behavior when it's not cued. Your Chihuahua should stop offering it freely and start to respond only to the cue. Just don't drop out the reinforcement too quickly. If the dog is unsure because your cue was conditioned too weakly, you could extinguish the behavior altogether. Go back to repetitions of labeling and reinforcing each sit for a few sessions to clear up your communication.

Initially, just get one cue, either verbal or a hand signal, under control and fluent. If you say the verbal cue while giving a hand signal at the same time, you run the risk of overshadowing or blocking, two common phenomena that are byproducts of unclear conditioning.

Overshadowing occurs when you present too many stimuli in the equation, and one that is unintended is linked to the behavior you're trying to get under control. For example, you lure a sit with a hand motion, and at the same time you say sit, while you are standing up, making eye contact, and leaning toward the dog. Which of these cues do you think the dog is learning means sit? Probably not the verbal one. More than likely it's the motion when standing up and making eye contact, or it could be the hand movement or leaning toward the dog.

Can you blame the dog for being confused? You are not clearly indicating what cue should be linked to the behavior. Beginner dog trainers have to learn to pay attention to all those extra body cues they throw into the mix, and then quiet their bodies, making their movements clear and deliberate and their verbal cues consistent.

Blocking refers to what happens when the handler is presenting a new cue, maybe a word, at the same time as a known cue like a hand signal. If you present them together, the dog blocks out the relevance of the new cue and just responds to the known cue. Instead, remember that you must present the new cue before the known cue. For example, if the dog has initially learned to follow a hand signal to sit, you would say the verbal cue, immediately but separately use the hand signal, and then reinforce the result. Then as your Chihuahua starts to anticipate and respond to the new verbal cue, you can drop out the use of the hand cue. Of course, you can retain the hand signal by reinforcing hand signal sits during other repetitions. Just don't use both cues simultaneously.

Now that you have your Chihuahua responding to the sit cue, and the behavior is under some control, you are going to introduce the next level of criteria, namely, to hold the position until signaled that the exercise is over. How will the dog know how long to stay in position, if he doesn't know when he is done? The signal that the exercise is over is called a release cue, and it's critical to the success of a solid sit and stay. Stay is simply the time interval between the sit and the release cue!

To teach the concept of waiting for release, begin to delay your click for a second or two when you ask your Chihuahua to sit. Once you have a significant duration, maybe ten seconds or more, you will switch over to using a release word while you drop off use of the clicker. You will replace the clicker with the release cue, but you should continue to reinforce

each repetition of the behavior with a quick presentation of the food for the time being.

Start by cueing your Chihuahua to move into sit position. Make eye contact, then say your release cue, a short word like "OK!", to the dog just before you click and throw your treat. This is similar to switching over from one cue to another as described above. The release cue will very quickly mean "you're done with that behavior and can come get your reinforcement." Once your Chihuahua is releasing fluently when you say the verbal release cue, you can start to drop out use of the clicker. Just don't forget to present the actual reinforcer, too.

Now that your Chihuahua is holding position and listening for the release cue, start to vary the amount of time your Chihuahua must hold position. You are not going to give an additional cue to mean stay—you have told the dog what to do, sit, and will teach him to hold position until told otherwise. Initially, you will hold position and release within a few seconds. Very quickly, you will begin to increase the duration, bringing it up to holding position for two to three minutes at a time.

It's critical, however, that you are careful as you build your duration. If your Chihuahua is breaking the position before you give the release cue, you are pushing the behavior too long! Pay careful attention to your Chihuahua's distraction level. If he is sniffing the ground at fifteen seconds, how can you ask for twenty-five seconds before release? You must increase the time intervals slowly upward, while at the same time the duration stays variable.

FOUNDATION SKILLS FOR EVERY CHIHUAHUA

A typical session would be as follows: Hold position for two seconds, five seconds, fifteen seconds, five seconds, ten seconds. The next series would be five seconds, fifteen seconds, twenty-five seconds, ten seconds, fifteen seconds. With each set of repetitions, you increase the average time that the dog must hold position. Once your Chihuahua can hold position for up to a minute or so, you are ready to move on to the final stage of training the sit, generalizing it to all the places you can think of!

To generalize the behavior to all contexts, move from room to room, inside to outside, from familiar place to unfamiliar place. You should be changing position too, starting out standing, but also sitting, lying down, and turning around to face away from the dog! When your Chihuahua gets ten in a row correct, move to the next location.

This is also the ideal time to transfer stimulus control to other people in the household that will need compliance from the dog. For example, as you go from room to room, switch off dog handling with your spouse, other family members, or a friend. Have them cue the sit and then release the dog, then give them a treat to give the dog. You want your Chihuahua to know that all humans know the rules of the game, not just the person who has the treats and a clicker.

As you move to new environments, expect the pup to be a bit slower or foggy, wondering if the previous rules for this behavior apply in the new location. This is completely normal. Go ahead and explain that "sit means sit" everywhere by starting easy and train up to the pup's present level of expertise in each new location.

Once your Chihuahua has the new behavior established in a variety of environments, will follow the cue from different people, and is calmly holding position until released, it's time to move away from the training context and use your puppy's skills in real life. Many dogs are never able to get to this stage, because most beginning trainers skip over this step, not realizing that the dog doesn't generalize what they've learned in training session to all environments and contexts. The dog gets stuck in a void. He needs a training context, complete with clicker and treats, to do the behavior, and the trainer is frustrated with an incomplete behavior that can't be used. It's now just a party trick.

Probably the most difficult step when generalizing a behavior for your Chihuahua is moving away from using predictable, continuous schedule reinforcement such as food, and applying real-life reinforcers like fun stuff, toys, access to attention or resources, or whatever else your Chihuahua likes to work for or appreciates, on an intermittent schedule as described in Chapter 9. You will never drop the rate to zero, or the behavior will extinguish, but it reinforcement should be presented just frequently enough to maintain the behavior.

So, how do you know your Chihuahua is ready? If your Chihuahua is reliable with the cue for sit and release for several sessions, successful at least 90 percent of the time, and the behavior is completely under stimulus control and well generalized, you can start to add in alternate reinforcers. You can release and play, or release and give tummy rubs, or release and open the back door. Move on to the next repetition, mixing in food, toys, attention, or access to fun stuff like favorite people or other pets as reinforcement after the release.

There you have it. The sit and stay, from start to finish. You have introduced the behavior, established a cue, generalized the sit and stay to all locations and other people, and switched the reinforcement to real life. Now you can move on to the next behavior!

Down and Stay

Now that your Chihuahua is sitting still and relaxed for more than a millisecond, what else should you teach? A natural segue would be to down or relax on cue when you need that extra bit of control, or when sent to a mat or bed.

Not only is it a more comfy position for your Chihuahua for an extended period of time, but your Chihuahua is also less likely to pop out of position without being released. When lying down, a dog is generally at a lower arousal level and more relaxed. Of course, not all small dogs appreciate this position, as it makes an already tiny breed feel a bit more vulnerable, so only use it in safe, relaxed settings.

Just as when training the sit position, you can either lure or shape the down position. To start shaping, begin in the most boring room of the home, making sure there are minimal distractions for your Chihuahua, such as toys or other people to pester. This can be a home office, laundry room, or even the bathroom. Go in with your clicker and treats in a pocket, shut the door, and sit down. Read a magazine, check your voice mail,

pass the time while you ignore the dog. Eventually, the bored dog will lie down, so click and treat!

If your Chihuahua stays in the down position for several seconds, try to deliver the food while the dog is in the down position. If your Chihuahua jumps up when you click, go back to the boring stuff. Eventually she'll stop staring at you, barking, or otherwise trying to get your attention, and lie down. Capture this one with your click, too, and don't forget to follow up with your treat! After the first few repetitions, your Chihuahua will be on to your game and will start to recycle those downs as fast as you can click.

An alternate method is to lure the dog into position. This isn't as straightforward as you might think, since your Chihuahua is already so close to the ground! Begin by placing a high-value treat in your closed hand. Cue your Chihuahua to sit, and then drop the hand to the floor directly in front of his front feet.

As your Chihuahua's nose approaches the floor to follow, pull the hand toward you on the floor. It should be an L-shaped motion from the dog's face to the floor a few feet in front of him. Think of your hand and the dog's nose as two magnets. If you go too fast, you will break the bond, but if you go at just the right speed the hand magnet will pull the nose magnet along with it. Click and treat as your Chihuahua's chest touches the floor, and then repeat the exercise.

As the dog starts to gain confidence in the position, don't forget you must fade out that hand lure or it will become part of the cue. One way is to lure the motion, then quickly move your hand behind your

back and click your Chihuahua for staying in position as you take your hand away.

A second lure method that is often preferred for tiny dogs is to place them on a low piece of furniture such as a bench or ottoman, a sturdy cardboard box, or a low step. Lure the dog by dropping your hand below the edge of the structure your Chihuahua is standing on, and he will have to fold up those tiny legs to reach the tidbit, and his belly will reach the support. Click and treat as soon as his belly touches the bottom! Practice on the furniture until the dog is recycling the down, and then move it onto the floor.

Another quick and easy way to jump start the down is the tunnel method. Sit on the floor, with your feet flat and knees up. Make a little tunnel under your legs and lure your Chihuahua's front end under your propped up knees, which must be low enough to make the dog crouch to get the treat. If the dog is on your right side, use your left hand to pull him

through the tunnel from right to left. Lure further and further under your legs, until your Chihuahua must be all the way down to reach the prize! Click and treat each of the approximations, and don't forget to jackpot when he is down.

FIVE TOP SKILLS TO TEACH YOUR CHIHUAHUA

Remember, never force your Chihuahua to down by pushing down on his back, pulling his feet out from under him, or looming over him. He will become startled and refuse to down, potentially becoming frightened or aggressive in the process. Do not tell the dog to down or stay in position yet, just click, treat, and immediately move on to the next repetition. Once your Chihuahua is recycling or "throwing" the behavior at you to make you click, you can delay the click and treat for a few seconds at a time as you begin to start your duration for the down and stay.

Once your Chihuahua is quickly recycling through the downs, add your label to the behavior, just as you did with the sit exercise. First label the behavior "Down" as your Chihuahua moves into position for thirty repetitions. Then for the next thirty repetitions begin to say the cue to the dog a millisecond before he moves into position, and for the final set, back it up until the cue is coming before the behavior. After this stage, do not click and treat if you haven't asked for the behavior. Do not tell your Chihuahua to stay, just delay the release a little longer for each repetition as you start to build your stay duration.

You can also introduce a hand signal for the down position if desired. Give your hand signal, usually a sweeping motion of the hand toward the floor, just before you say the previously conditioned verbal cue. Then hold, click and treat as above. Your Chihuahua will quickly associate the hand signal with the verbal cue, and start to move on presentation of the hand signal. Drop your verbal cue, and then hold, click and treat with a jackpot of high-value treats! Never use the verbal and hand cues

together, you will cause confusion and neither one will give you good stimulus control. Instead, teach them both, and then use them alternately.

Just as with training your Chihuahua to sit and stay, you will teach your Chihuahua that he should hold the down position until released. Once the dog is committed to the position, staying in position for five to ten seconds or even more while staying relaxed and calm, you will make eye contact, say your release cue "OK!" in a happy, relaxed tone, then click and treat. Very quickly, your Chihuahua will realize this is just like the sit release and will start to listen for the cue to move out of position.

Once your Chihuahua is responding to the verbal release cue, you can start to drop out use of the clicker as a marker. Don't forget to continue to follow up each release with reinforcement for the time being. If you drop out the reinforcement, the behavior will extinguish altogether. As with the sit, you will begin to increase the duration the dog stays down, bringing it up to holding for two to three minutes at a time.

So now you have the down on cue, your Chihuahua is comfortably holding position for several minutes until released, and you are ready to take it out of the classroom. Time to play "Where in the World" with your Chihuahua again!

Begin to practice the downs and releases in new places every session, and don't forget to change your position, too. You don't want to get stuck with a dog that can only down when you are face-to-face. Practice while sitting, standing, facing away from the dog, and while you are moving around the room.

When practicing in the new places, be prepared to start with an easy duration and build it up to the current duration a few seconds at a time. It's typical for the distractions of new places to interrupt the progress of training the behavior. Expect to train up the duration of the behavior in each new location as you go through this exercise, and be prepared to release the dog before he gets too distracted or anxious.

This is also the stage that you will generalize the down cue to other people. Have family and friends get involved in your training, or else your Chihuahua will not understand to follow basic cues from other people.

To start, have a friend or training partner give the down cue, release after a short easy duration, and immediately drop a high-value reinforcer. Help your partner with the timing and with maintaining consistent cues. If you are telling the dog to "Down" as a cue, and your training partner says "Lay down!", your Chihuahua will become confused.

Once your Chihuahua is fluent in the down position you will begin to mix in other kinds of reinforcers. Remember that though you will often use high-value tidbits in the training, you will not always have a clicker and treats with you. You need to become adept at finding ways to reinforce good behavior with things other than food.

The quickest way to introduce other kinds of reinforcement into the game is as follows: Start by reinforcing ten downs in a row by clicking and treating. For the next set, you will release, reinforcing nine with the food and one with something else your Chihuahua loves. For example, after releasing your Chihuahua from the down you can toss his favorite toy, play a favorite game, or give your Chihuahua his favorite type of petting. With small Chihuahuas that love contact, you can even use picking them up as a reinforcer.

Continue dropping out the food reinforcement like this, until you can reinforce nine downs with something else and just one with the food. You should now be substituting other reinforcers regularly in your training and maintaining the down position for several minutes at a time, in a variety of locations, with the occasional high-value food treat.

Easy Loose-Leash Walking

Don't be fooled by the title, loose-leash walking may be the most difficult exercise you will attempt in training your Chihuahua and takes both time and patience. Unfortunately, it is also the behavior that degrades the quickest if you accidentally reinforce poor behavior or change your criteria because you're unsure of what you want.

Before taking at crack at this, take some time to think about what you want for your Chihuahua's leash walking skills. You probably know what you don't want your dog doing—pulling on the leash, choking himself in his hurry to get somewhere, or lagging behind you, timid and sad. Randomly weaving between your legs, erratic changes of direction, and biting the leash as you walk are probably no-no's, too.

So, what are the behaviors you are looking for? Walking calmly on your left side, with a loose leash, and gracefully adjusting to your pace and change of direction is a good place to start. You want to easily manage your Chihuahua on leash, keeping him under control without worrying about tripping, stepping on him, or choking him as you walk down the street.

Start with introducing your Chihuahua to a comfortable buckle collar, or a harness, with a lightweight six-foot leash attached. If this is the first session wearing a collar or harness, you can just click and treat your dog for standing next to you while wearing his spiffy new gear! When

he is comfortable with and ignoring the new stuff and watching you expectantly, you can practice a few sits and downs on leash as a way to warm him up and let him know its training time.

Start the loose-leash walk training standing still. It may sound silly, but if your Chihuahua can't keep the leash relaxed and stay focused while you stand still, he can't do it while you're moving. For the first session it doesn't matter what else your pup is doing; your only concern is whether or not the lead is loose while you're standing there.

It's also a good idea to begin your practice after the dog has had a bit of exercise but is not too exhausted to pay attention. If your Chihuahua has been cooped up all day and bored, it's a good idea to let him burn off some of that energy so he is not so easily distractible.

One way to help position the dog correctly is the "cookie magnet." Pretend your left hand is one magnet and his nose is another magnet. Steadily lure the dog to your left side with the cookie magnet, click, and release the treat just as he is facing forward and in line with your left knee, a position we sometimes call the "sweet spot." If you go too fast, you'll break the magnet bond, and if you go too high he will jump to get your hand.

You can alternately have the pup target your left hand, your finger, or a target stick if he is familiar with target training, clicking and treating him when he lines up in the sweet spot. Either of these methods will give your Chihuahua a visual cue as to where he should be to get reinforcement and can then be faded out once he finding that sweet spot on his own.

Once your Chihuahua is paying attention, and the leash is loose, and he's in the sweet spot, you can introduce movement. Start in a relatively distraction-free location, initially. You can even begin indoors or on a back porch or deck. Cheerfully say "Let's go!" and take two steps forward, using your hand lure to keep the dog with you. Click as he moves forward, and deliver your treat right next to your left knee.

Continue to click and treat for forward movement a few steps at a time, always saying "Let's go!" before you move—this will become your cue for moving forward. Do not use the leash to tug the pup into position. Instead, lure the dog, using your

cookie magnet if you have to, or just capture it with your clicker. Every few steps, you will click as he's in the sweet spot, and then deliver your treat next to your left leg, building the number of steps between clicks over several sessions.

As you move forward, your Chihuahua might get distracted and maybe zoom out to the end of the leash in front of you. You have two choices: your can either stop moving forward, and teach the dog that the leash must stay loose to get anywhere, or you can change direction, teaching the dog to follow your lead because you become silly and unpredictable when he's not paying attention.

If you choose to stop moving when the leash is tight, you will have to lure him back to the sweet spot and move forward several steps before you click and treat. Sometimes, this method is like herding a cat—not very effective if you don't have good luring skills and patience. Of course, if you do this a few times successfully, it makes the criteria very clear for your Chihuahua, and it only takes a few repetitions for him to get it.

The second method will rely on you paying attention very closely. The second your Chihuahua moves forward out of the sweet spot, but before the leash is tight, you will cue "Let's go!" and carefully change direction. Do not yank the dog off his feet, just use the "Let's go!" to indicate you're about to do something different. Repeat this every time he forges ahead, and very quickly he will start watching you, just in case you go off course again.

Aim for several short sessions of loose-leash walking a day. You will add a few steps to your skills each day. Begin to practice turns and vary your speed once your Chihuahua can do fifteen or twenty steps forward and not lose attention.

Give yourself plenty of opportunity to keep things under control as you practice. Every few steps you should be stopping and cue a sit or down and then release the dog to go sniff, play, or explore. As your skills improve, you can increase the number of steps between stops for play and sniffing.

Don't forget to fade out use of the clicker once the leash walking is highly reliable. Start by walking forward a few steps and coming to a halt. Cue a sit, and then release the dog from a sit position, and immediately treat. Never release while moving; things will degrade quickly as your Chihuahua will start releasing himself as you move along. Once the dog is sitting and waiting for the release cue from the heel position, start dropping out the click and treat, and begin substituting real-life reinforcement, just as in previous exercises.

A favorite method for teaching good leash walking behavior is to skip use of a leash altogether. This is the method of choice for many trainers, and must be started in a contained area, but once you have polished your skills off leash, moving to an area that requires a leash for safety will be a snap.

Start by showing your Chihuahua a treat from your left hand, or offer a hand target, and start walking briskly in a large circle to the right. Ignore the pup until he catches up with you and is in that sweet spot on your left side, then click and treat. No cues or signals are given to the pup, it's up to him to figure out how to get you to reinforce his behavior.

Once your Chihuahua is finding the position on his own when you start moving, add your "Let's go!" cue. Begin to change pace in the circle, sometimes slowing down and sometimes speeding up. Spiral your big circle down to a tiny one, where you almost pivot in place. Add in changes of direction, and even teach the dog to heel on your right side, a skill that will come in handy if you plan to do obedience, Rally, or agility training later.

The Recall

"Come on cue." "Come fast, come now, and come when I call you one time." "Come no matter what you're doing, who your playing with, or what other distractions are around." That's an advanced skill to train your Chihuahua to do, but it can save your Chihuahua's life one day. Don't skimp on this one! This is one behavior that you should practice throughout the lifetime of your Chihuahua, for that one-split-second emergency that may occur.

Training your Chihuahua to come on cue, called a recall, is really no different from training any other behavior. It requires building a rock-solid foundation built on tiny increments of criteria, which is then generalized to other locations. It's very easy to train a recall, but the challenge comes in setting up the levels of criteria so the dog can learn to be reliable in heavy distractions, during stressful moments, or when he's just busy doing something else.

Many people train in lumps of criteria. They teach the dog to come, then they want to immediately jump to come fast, now, and from across the yard while

there's a cat teasing you. Not so fast—that sets the dog up for failure and the handler up for frustration, because the dog cannot comply at that level of difficulty.

Instead you have to train by splitting your criteria into smaller pieces. Teach the recall from two feet away, then five feet away, then work up to a distance of up to twenty feet, with no distractions. Then review the recall from five feet, but slowly add in one or two distractions, maybe just a movement by the handler, or simple changes in position. Work back out to twenty feet with those distractions. Then change locations, but go back to five-foot recalls, working out to twenty feet again, slowly adding in those distractions you know your Chihuahua can handle.

The other important component of a reliable recall is the association the dog

has made with the cue. "Fido, Come!" must be conditioned so strongly your Chihuahua thinks he won the lotto every time he hears that word.

It's incredibly easy to change that association to a negative, if you cue the dog to come and then introduce something even mildly aversive, say, putting on a leash at the park when your Chihuahua isn't keen on going home yet. So, it's critical to get the cue well generalized and under control, without making negative associations.

In this exercise, we will back-chain the behavior, meaning we will teach the end of the behavior first. This makes the series of behaviors strongest near the end, and even more reinforcing for the dog to do. Initially, you start labeling the position of sitting toe to toe and making eye contact as "Fido, Come!" for the dog. Over several sessions, it will come to mean that wherever he is, whatever he is doing, when he hears those magic words he should assume that position because great things will happen for him.

Start recall training in a contained area, with no distractions. You need to be the most fabulous thing in the room! Get his attention and take a step or two backward. He will probably follow along with you and may sit in front of you, waiting to see what's next. Say "Fido, Come!", make soft eye contact, then click and treat! That's it!

After several repetitions take a few more giant steps backward and repeat. The dog will probably move with you, and you should be dispensing high-value reinforcers as fast as he can get to you.

Continue to add steps to the exercise, still practicing in a contained area with minimal distractions. Move backward, sideways, and turn around and walk across the room. Change your position from standing to sitting to kneeling, each time saying "Fido, Come!" just as the dog sits in front of you and makes eye contact. You can have your training partner gently hold the dog to give you time to move away, and release the dog's collar just as you say "Fido, Come!" in a cheerful voice. You want your Chihuahua to be running to you as fast as those little legs can get there!

Begin practicing face-to-face recalls in a number of settings, moving to a new location in the house every few repetitions. Gradually increase the distance the dog must move toward you to get clicked, still on leash or contained. Only call the pup when you are 99-percent sure he will be successful by carefully managing the environmental distractions. Then begin to practice outdoors, first on a leash, then off leash in a contained area, then on a long line in an unfenced area.

Additionally, start to vary the amount of time the dog should sit facing you before he gets clicked. You don't want to turn this into tag, where your Chihuahua checks in and immediately scoots off to do something else more fun. Remember to call in a cheerful voice, and when he sits in front of you, to get the click and treat, the pup must be close enough that you can reach down and touch the collar.

Remember, everyone in the house must go through this process. It is unsafe to assume your Chihuahua will come to anyone who has not already successfully practiced this behavior with the dog, or if you have not generalized the cue to include everyone.

Once the recall means "run over and sit in front of me," begin to add random real-life recalls. Several times a day, do a short-distance surprise recall when your Chihuahua is engaged with something else, perhaps playing with a person or another dog, chewing toys, sniffing a tree, or in other words, just being a dog. When he gets there, click and jackpot these recalls, and then immediately release your Chihuahua to go back to what he was doing. Releasing the dog back to his previous activity is an incredibly potent reinforcer and will help avoid teaching the dog that recalls are a signal that all the fun is done.

This stage really helps your Chihuahua generalize this cue, as it will now pop up in real life, not just in training sessions. Remember you must be prepared to reinforce, or don't use the cue yet. This is still a training setup and you should be prepared!

Once you have a strongly conditioned recall in very controlled situations, you can make it more challenging. A typical progression of the "Fido, Come!" cue over several weeks might be as follows:

Come now
Come fast
Come from across the room when
　you're not looking at me
Come from another room
Come to whoever calls you
Come if you're busy with a bone or toy
Come if you're being petted by
　someone else
Come if you're sleeping
Come if you're barking at the cat
Come if you're playing with your
　Chihuahua friend
Come if you're eating (JACKPOT)

In all of these levels, your Chihuahua would be heavily reinforced for the recall and then released to continue what she was doing. Now reestablish the recall outdoors, starting from the beginning level, each time ending with a sit in front of you, followed by click and treat! Then reestablish the recall at someone else's house. Then reestablish in a distracting and exciting place like the park.

Begin to fade out using the clicker to mark the recall once it's highly reliable, meaning your Chihuahua is responsive to the cue at least 95 percent of the time. A quick method is to do a series of ten recalls, and replace one click with a release, deliver your reinforcement, and then just cue the next repetition. On the next series, drop out two random clicks. Continue dropping out clicks over several sessions until you can keep the behavior going without clicking any repetitions.

Always make recalls rewarding and use the highest value reinforcer at your disposal. Sometimes that will be food, but it can also be the opportunity to return to playing with a doggy playmate, getting busy with a bone, or playing a rousing game of chase.

Most important, remember, never recall your Chihuahua to scold, reprimand, or punish. If you must do something aversive, such as giving medicine, clipping toenails, or anything else your Chihuahua doesn't like, you go to the dog rather than have the dog come to you. Your Chihuahua's life could be in jeopardy if you link recalls to punishment or aversive handling.

11 *Five Skills for Great Manners*

Finding Your Behavior Boundaries

Living with a Chihuahua can be a wonderful experience. Sometimes, living with a Chihuahua can be a nightmare. Which type of experience you have largely depends on your ability to set reasonable limits on what's appropriate behavior for your Chihuahua, be consistent with your direction, and then maintain good behavior for the long term. In other words, teaching your Chihuahua good manners will make living with your Chihuahua easy and fun, allow him to participate in household and social activities, and will improve the relationship between your Chihuahua and your guests.

Who's There? Front Door Behavior

When working on front door manners, do not get so concerned about what you don't want, perhaps manic barking, hysterical jumping, and demanding attention from guests, that you lose sight of what you do want. If your Chihuahua's front door manners aren't where they should be, or you just want to get started on the right foot with a new puppy, start to prioritize what you think a dog with good manners looks like. These dogs are usually calm with all four feet on the floor, or sitting, maybe alert barking once or twice and then stopping when requested, and then offering polite greetings when appropriate, without crowding or demanding attention. Dogs with good manners didn't get them by themselves, someone trained them to be that way.

So, how do you teach such good manners to your Chihuahua? Start by defining your end goal. Is it to have a dog that stays relaxed and stays under control with direction from the handler, while strangers enter the home, visit, and exit the home? As you practice this exercise, reactive or highly aroused adult dogs can learn that entering strangers are not a threat, and young puppies can learn that having strangers come into the house is a calm, rewarding social experience and no reason to get aroused or upset.

To start with, you will practice front door behavior without opening the door.

Put a leash on your Chihuahua, letting him drag it around the house as you go about your daily activities. Go to the front door and knock on the inside. Your Chihuahua will probably come to check out who's here! No matter how your Chihuahua reacts to the knocking, pick up the leash and calmly cue your Chihuahua to sit when he gets there.

Hold the sit position for ten or more seconds, click and treat and then walk away from the front door. If your

Chihuahua already has a solid sit-stay with release you can cue the dog to sit, hold it and then release.

You should also practice this with the doorbell, having a partner ring the bell at variable intervals. Repeat this exercise for enough repetitions until your Chihuahua predictably comes to you at the front door and can sit quietly, waiting for direction, when he hears the knock or doorbell. You are working on changing the cue of knocking or door bell ringing from "get aroused" to "get calm."

Once your Chihuahua is holding position, you can add the next stage. When your Chihuahua sits, reach for and then open the door. If your Chihuahua pops up from his seated position, immediately shut the door! If your Chihuahua breaks his sit as you reach for the doorknob, withdraw your hand from the doorknob and calmly tell him to sit.

Then try it again. Get busy doing something else, then go knock on the door, reach for the doorknob, and open the door, releasing your Chihuahua after you shut the door. Repeat this exercise many times, and then practice the sequence using the doorbell.

After you have established the front door as a place to remain calm and under control, you will start to introduce one new person at a time into the exercise until your Chihuahua is comfortable with a group of people coming into the home, moving around, and exiting the home. These exercises are always done with high-value treats. Have several bags ready to go, each containing tiny pieces of chopped hot dogs, chicken, cheese, liver, or steak. A variety of treats is even better.

Your Chihuahua should be on leash during this exercise. Have the helper ring the bell or knock on the door. You should approach the door, directing your Chihuahua just as in previous exercises. You will open the door just as before, but this time someone (the helper) is standing there! The helper should enter, but should ignore your Chihuahua, not making eye contact or saying anything, and not touching your Chihuahua, while you direct the dog to stay in position. If your Chihuahua pops up, the helper should immediately exit and close the door.

Work up to having the helper enter, say hello to you, and perhaps even come into the home and settle into a chair or at the table, all while ignoring the dog. You should keep the arousal level low and

continue to direct the dog's behavior while he remains on leash. Each stage may need several sessions to get the behavior fluent.

When you have practiced having the helper enter, sit for a few minutes, get up and leave while your Chihuahua is calm, you can then release the dog while the helper is still there to go say a low-key hello. Coach each helper not to pet, play with, or pay attention to a dog that is jumping, barking, or getting aroused. Before the visitor gets up to move toward the door, call your Chihuahua back to you, pick up his leash, and instruct him to sit. Reinforce the calm sit while the visitor moves toward the door.

As you move through the stages, begin practicing with family, then close friends, then guests your dog doesn't know;

coach the helper that they should not overwhelm your Chihuahua with over-the-top greetings, petting, or rewarding bad manners. If they start playing with him or petting him while he's hyped up to demand attention, he will regress, and pretty soon will be barking, jumping, and an overall pest when guests arrive.

Occasionally, the front door has become a place that results in outright aggression. If your dog shows signs of impending threat when people enter the front door, or if your dog has already bitten someone, manage the environment by moving your Chihuahua to a location she can relax in when friends are entering the home. An overly aroused or aggressive dog is not having a good time when guests arrive,

she is upset. You will need to get hands-on help from a behaviorist or certified dog trainer to design a modification program to address your dog's underlying associations with people before you can train appropriate front door behavior.

Stop Begging!

Forlorn looks, with big sad eyes. A subtle whine, some barking and perhaps a hopeful tail wag when you look his way, or a paw scratching on your leg. Someone has done a great job of training your Chihuahua to beg. That's right, poor table manners were learned, initially reinforced when someone slipped a tasty tidbit to a begging dog because they thought it was cute, or thought it would make the behavior stop once the dog got what he was begging for. It's not too late, however, to change this embarrassing behavior.

It's only natural to want to give your Chihuahua the occasional tidbit. After all, food is how we celebrate with family and friends, and it's at the center of home life, so of course we will want to include our four-legged family member in family dinners, holidays, and other celebrations. Of course, how you share that tidbit is what makes all the difference in your Chihuahua's behavior during mealtimes.

Stopping the behavior is a relatively straightforward process, theoretically. If the behaviors of sad eyes and a low whine stop paying off for your Chihuahua, he will stop those behaviors. Ignoring the dog completely at mealtimes will prevent begging or stop it when it does occur. Of course, if someone slips Fido the occasional tasty tidbit from the table, even if it happens once, it will actually strengthen the behavior because it's being intermittently reinforced. Now, he's playing the table tidbit lottery!

For any real success at tackling the begging behavior, it's important to set up rules that everyone can reasonably comply with. If most of the family is ignoring your Chihuahua during meals to extinguish the begging behavior, but Grandpa is still slipping the dog something under the table, he is undermining all of the other training.

The most effective method combines reinforcement of an incompatible behavior with extinction of the actual table begging behaviors. Sit down for dinner, with the agreement that everyone will completely ignore your Chihuahua while they eat their meal, with one person keeping an eye on the dog. Have someone at the table set aside any tiny tidbits, as long as they are healthy and safe for dogs, that they would like to share to use for this exercise.

Your Chihuahua, of course, will initially put on his best show, begging like his life depends on it. He's convinced he is starving to death and is trying to convince you, too.

He will try everything he knows, including at some point backing up, sitting, or lying down away from the table. Bingo! This is the time that someone will get up, put a small jackpot of goodies in the dog's dish, and then come back to the table.

Now your Chihuahua has just been reinforced for not begging. Hmm, maybe

he will try that again. Time for the next repetition. Continue to ignore Fido and eat your meal, putting aside a just-right reward for the next time. Wait for Fido to back up from the table, lie down, or otherwise do something that is not pesky and rude. Jackpot in the dish, away from the table! Make sure everyone gets a chance to practice during the course of the meal, even Grandpa.

Once your Chihuahua catches on to the new game, you can start to shape a more specific behavior. Many people shape the dog to lie in his bed, or on a mat. Sometimes just staying away from the table can be their criteria. Some people don't mind if Fido sits under the table, they just don't want whining and a tiny paw scratching their guests' legs.

You are now shaping good behavior by rewarding your Chihuahua for polite behaviors, while you ignore the pushy behavior. The pesky behavior you ignore will disappear, sometimes quite dramatically. The behavior you're rewarding will strengthen and get repeated. Grandpa still gets to give his tidbits, and your Chihuahua will learn to calmly wait at your feet while you eat your meal and will patiently wait for his tiny tidbit. Everyone is happy.

As his manners become established, you will then start to reward less frequently and then only occasionally. You will gradually switch from giving something at each meal, to one tidbit after the occasional special meal. Now your Chihuahua is playing the lottery again, so make it worth his while, and you will strengthen and maintain the new, nonbegging behavior during mealtimes.

Attention-Seeking Behaviors: Barking, Nipping, and Jumping

Your Chihuahua may display a cluster of annoying behaviors that often occur together: barking at you, nipping at you, or jumping on you, demanding your attention. Remember, dogs do what works for them, and reinforcement for behavior comes from every interaction you have with your Chihuahua, whether you are training or not.

Many of the persistent attention-seeking behaviors have been accidentally reinforced enough to establish and maintain them over long periods of time. Behavior charting is an excellent method to help you to recognize and change your reaction to these behaviors, decreasing their reinforcement value for your Chihuahua.

First, you must figure out which behaviors are getting reinforced. How does your Chihuahua elicit attention from you? If you are not sure, spend a day observing and writing down when you react to your Chihuahua and what behavior initiated this reaction. Typical attention-seeking behaviors are barking at you, nipping at you, jumping up or pawing you, or nudging your hands with a tiny nose.

After you have made a list of all of the ways your Chihuahua demands attention, select the most prevalent one to modify first. You are ready to make your chart, listing the days of the week on the bottom and the typical number of solicitations on the side, starting at zero.

Behavior Chart

Number of instances of pawing for attention vs days of the week each instance occured. After a typical extinction burst on Wednesday, the behavior quickly dropped off, approaching zero by Sunday.

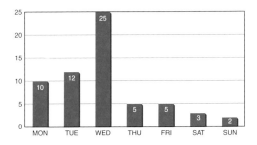

Behavior Chart Example

Use a chart to mark every time your Chihuahua exhibits the behavior to try to draw attention from you—but now, instead of responding to your Chihuahua, you will ignore him, get up, and go put a tally mark on your chart. The mark will go in the box that represents the behavior and the day it happened.

In as short as a week you will be amazed at the decrease in these attention-seeking behaviors. By ignoring them and moving away, you are no longer are rewarding the problem behaviors. Your Chihuahua perceives that these behaviors will no longer work to get your attention; they, in fact, result in you withdrawing your attention.

As you initiate this exercise, remember: Each time your Chihuahua seeks your attention with one of the listed behaviors,

you will get up, walk over to the chart, and put a mark in the appropriate day. Each family member also has to participate in the charting exercise. Initially, you will catch yourself accidentally giving the requested attention—that's okay; it takes time and patience to change behavior.

Choose one behavior to focus on for a full week. Evaluate the decrease in frequency, and then choose whether to move to the next behavior or keep charting the same one. Occasionally a behavior is so entrenched you may need to chart for a second week. That's fine, it will just be a more gradual extinction.

Begin by picking the most frequent or bothersome behavior. With this method, you will quickly see a decrease in the number of times your Chihuahua elicits your attention with this particular behavior. Once the old behavior is begins to dramatically decrease you should start to reinforce the new "good" behavior. For example, if your previously barking dog starts to come to you and sits quietly, you must reinforce the sitting quietly. Don't skip this stage or your Chihuahua will just insert the behavior of his choice, usually an even worse one like jumping up or nipping.

When doing any type of behavior modification activity such as this, it is normal for behaviors to get worse before they get better. This is because what has always worked for your Chihuahua is suddenly no longer working, so he will actively try to push it to the point that it works again. It will get more intense and occur more frequently just before it changes and gets better. This is called an extinction burst. Be patient and hang in there—you will see results!

12 *Five Fun Things to Teach Your Chihuahua*

Trick-Training as a Boredom Buster

Sometimes pet owners hit a roadblock with their training program and often trick-training is the answer. It is an ideal way to hone your training skills without the pressure of getting it perfect, and it's a great way to keep your dog's mind and body occupied while teaching him how to work with you. Trick training also requires almost no space or equipment, doesn't depend on the weather being just right, and is an overall boredom buster. Mostly, it's about fun though, and Chihuahuas love to play games! Here are some of the easiest tricks to train.

Targeting

Targeting is one of the first clicker skills to teach puppies, because it is so much fun but it's also a wonderful way to teach an older dog the clicker game. It's often a foundation skill used as a base for building other behaviors, including positioning, leash walking, controlled jumping, crawling, and lots of other tricks. Once your Chihuahua is fluent in targeting, you'll find you use it for all sorts of things.

To get started, you will need a wooden spoon, a twelve-inch ruler, a 24-inch wooden dowel, or maybe a magic wand. You can even use your index finger. Pretty much anything long and pointy will do. To increase interest rub something interesting on the end, maybe peanut butter or cream cheese.

Hold the target out in front or slightly to one side of you. Make it look interesting, but don't wave or point it at your Chihuahua; it might look too much like a weapon. Most dogs will investigate this new and yummy-smelling thing, so when your dog extends his neck to sniff or lick the target stick, click and treat.

Repeat this initial presentation several times, and begin to move the stick a few inches at a time randomly. After the first few clicks you won't need to put a lure like peanut butter on the end. Just present the target, and wait for the touch.

You don't want a shy, whisper-soft nose touch, so shape it until your Chihuahua is confidently bumping the stick or your finger before you click. Also, only click the nose touching the stick if it is with a closed mouth. This is not a tug-of-war or fetch, and often the dog thinks he should put it in his mouth. If your Chihuahua grabs the stick, just hold it and wait for him to back off, then click when he approaches again without opening his mouth.

Be patient, just present the stick or your finger and let your Chihuahua come to it, do not bring it to him. If the dog is shy, you can warm him up by holding the target stick right in front of him and clicking when he stretches his neck, but then move it one inch forward for the next repetition. You are trying to get your Chihuahua to step toward the stick.

Move it higher, lower, right, and left. Turn around and do it in each direction, and on each side, holding the stick with your other hand. You know your Chihuahua is in the game when he starts to follow the stick wherever it goes!

Once your Chihuahua is thrilled to bump the target stick, you will put it on a verbal cue. You can begin to say "Touch!" in a happy voice just as you present the stick, and then click and treat when you feel the bump. After a session or two, he should be fluently touching the target stick when you cue it—after then, only click and treat for targeting the stick when you've cued it.

Now you can teach your Chihuahua to target other objects or people. Point to the other object or person with the hand you usually target with, and cue "Touch!" Initially, you may have to hold your hand right next to the object, but after a few repetitions, your Chihuahua will bump the object right next to your hand. Capture that with a click and treat, practice until it is fluent behavior, and then try another object. Impress your family by teaching your Chihuahua to touch objects in the room by name, or target specific people in a group!

Spinning

Teaching your Chihuahua to spin in a circle is a quick, cute, and easy trick to teach in just a few sessions. You can put an adorable cue on the spinning behavior like "Yahoo!" A fun cue might be "Wax On!" for a clockwise spin and "Wax Off!" for a counterclockwise spin. The trick can also be modified so the dog spins on his hind legs like a ballerina or stays on four legs to chase his tail.

Start by luring your Chihuahua in a circle with a target stick or hand target. Warm up the dog with a few easy target repetitions, and then begin to slowly move the target in a clockwise circle. If your Chihuahua follows the target all the way around, you will click and treat as your Chihuahua comes around to the start position.

If your Chihuahua is a bit tentative in following the target all the way around, you can click for approximations of the circle. A few clicks for a half circle will increase his confidence greatly. Some dogs have a preference as to which direction they spin, so if you run into some initial resistance, try spinning in the other direction.

If your Chihuahua doesn't know how to follow a target yet, you can use the "cookie magnet" by holding a tasty tidbit in your closed fist and placing it right in front of his nose. Imagine your fist and your Chihuahua's nose are two magnets, and gently lead him around the circle, nose first. Don't go too fast, or the magnet bond will break, and keep your hand low or the dog may jump up to follow it. With this method you will click when your Chihuahua comes around to the start of the circle as above, and then open your magnet hand and deliver the treat.

Once you have your Chihuahua following the target or cookie magnet in a circle you will start to shape your trick into something special. You can fade out your lure or target to a discrete hand signal, or put it on a cute and funny verbal cue.

Begin fading the target stick by simply making it shorter or holding it a little higher when you make the circle motion. Continue to make it smaller until it disappears in your hand and just your finger makes a little circle. If you are hand targeting or using a cookie magnet, stand up and hold your hand higher while you make the circle, and begin to make the motion smaller and less obvious. It will start to become a hand cue, rather than a lure. Eventually, perhaps, your hand cue may merely be an index-finger motion that is virtually imperceptible to casual observers—they will think the dog is telepathic!

After fading out the hand target, or turning it into a subtle hand cue, you can also give it a snazzy verbal cue. To condition your verbal cue for the spin, say the verbal cue just before you give the subtle hand signal to spin. Click and treat successful spins. After ten repetitions, your Chihuahua should be anticipating the hand signal when you say the verbal cue, so just skip the hand signal and see if the dog does the behavior. Click and jackpot this spin! If he didn't quite get it, go back and use the verbal cue followed by the subtle hand cue for another ten repetitions, then try again.

Once your Chihuahua is responding to the hand or verbal cue, you have generalized the trick to a variety of locations, and he can perform with it distractions, you can drop out use of the clicker. You will

cue the spin ten times in a row. Drop out one click, praise your Chihuahua, and cue the next repetition. Which click you drop out should be random. On the next set, you will drop out two or three clicks. Continue until your dog can do ten spins in a row, with no clicks at all. Just remember to reinforce at the end with something your Chihuahua does like, otherwise the behavior will stop altogether!

Crawl

Crawling is another cute and easy trick to train your Chihuahua to do. It's especially easy to train if your Chihuahua already knows how to down on cue and follow a target stick or touch a hand target.

Start with your Chihuahua in the down position. Offer the target right in front of the dog's front feet, keeping target low or on the ground. Click and treat your Chihuahua for reaching forward and touching the target or hand while in the down position. Start to move forward a half inch at a time so your dog has to stretch to the target, but not so far that he pops up and walks toward the target.

Do a series of easy touches, then pull the target just a tiny bit out of range. Your Chihuahua should move his body forward to hit the target, so click and jackpot! Once your Chihuahua is confidently moving forward to touch the target, begin to move it an inch at a time, until the dog is crawling the length of his body or more in the down position toward the target.

Of course, you will want to fade out the target to a discreet signal to crawl. You can quickly modify a hand target by

holding it a bit higher than the dog and making a sliding hand motion toward you. You can fade this signal further by standing up and holding your hand closer to your body or at your side, with the index finger still pointed down, and giving a tiny sweeping motion toward your body. Once your Chihuahua is responding to the subtle hand cue, you can introduce a theatrical verbal cue—perhaps something like "Duck!" just before you give the subtle hand cue to crawl forward.

A variation on this classic trick is to have your Chihuahua duck with his head down. When your Chihuahua is in the down position and you delay the click, without asking him to crawl forward, he will probably get bored and put his head on his paws. Click and treat this head motion a few times, instead of asking him to crawl forward, and give it a cue, since the head motion is a new behavior.

Now, start to ask for the head motion at the end of the crawl, so that your Chihuahua crawls forward on the crawl cue, and then puts his head down on his paws at the end. This variation is adorable if you want to do the trick as part of a sequence to give the crawl a dramatic ending.

Hoop Games

Hoop games can be a great way to exercise your Chihuahua indoors, as well as to teach some impressive tricks, with a minimal investment in props. Most toy stores will sell inexpensive plastic hoops in an assortment of flashy colors, and you can sometimes find them in various sizes from small to extra-large.

The simple trick begins with having your Chihuahua walk through the hoop with you holding one edge and the other edge resting on the ground. Position your Chihuahua to one side, and lure her through with a toy, or throw a treat through the hoop, clicking as she walks through to follow the treat. It can be helpful to hold the hoop next to a wall so your Chihuahua can't walk around to get the treat. Now, do it in the other direction, throwing a toy or treat through and clicking as the dog walks through the hoop.

Continue to click and treat anytime your Chihuahua walks through the hoop, and begin to raise it off the ground. You can keep it very low, having your

Chihuahua hop through the hoop an inch or so off the ground, and then increase the challenge for your Chihuahua; raise it up to eight inches off the ground. Keep in mind your Chihuahua's size and fitness level, and don't ask him to jump higher than is safe.

If at any time your Chihuahua walks under the hoop instead of hopping through, just lower it a bit, and continue to click and treat your Chihuahua for jumping through. Then try to raise it again.

Once your Chihuahua is hopping through, give the behavior a cute verbal cue like "Ta-da!" As your Chihuahua hops through, say the cue, and then immediately click and treat. Slowly back it up until you are saying it before the dog jumps through the hoop. Once the dog responds to the verbal cue, only click and treat the trick when you've given the cue first.

A dramatic variation on the hoop trick that is a bit more advanced is to have your Chihuahua jump through your arms. Start by having the dog walk and then jump through the hoop on-cue while you are kneeling.

Once your Chihuahua is used to your new body position, start to wrap your arms around the circumference of the hoop, making the circle smaller and smaller on each repetition. When you have brought your arms all the way around to form a complete circle, eliminate the plastic hoop.

It will be a bit intimidating for your Chihuahua to jump through the smaller circles so close to your body, so look away from the dog in the direction of his travel. Make sure you're not staring directly at your Chihuahua. You should also deliver a very high-value reinforcer or jackpot after the first few repetitions through your arms. While jumping through your arms will take more work than simply hopping through the hoop, it's a flashy and impressive trick to have in your Chihuahua's repertoire.

Crazy Eights

Weaving through your legs in a figure-eight pattern takes some skill, but it's an impressive trick that your Chihuahua will really enjoy doing. It can be done while you are stationary, or your dog can weave through your legs as you walk, sometimes called threading the needle.

Using a target stick is helpful for this trick, otherwise you will end up looking like a pretzel trying to hand target your Chihuahua through your own legs. If you haven't taught your Chihuahua to follow the target stick, go back to review it now.

First, you have to get your Chihuahua comfortable moving between your legs. Start with your Chihuahua sitting facing you, with your legs open, shoulder width. Hold your target stick straight down your back toward the ground, so your Chihuahua sees it behind you through your open legs. Tell your Chihuahua to touch the target stick, and click as he moves through your legs toward the stick; throw the treat behind you. Practice this step for ten or more repetitions until he is confidently moving through your open legs.

For the next set, you will cue your Chihuahua to go through your legs again. As he moves toward the target stick, you will circle it to your left side and stop when you get to the heel position. Click and treat when your Chihuahua comes around your leg to your left side. Now he is facing the same direction as you.

Now, you will show your Chihuahua your right hand as a target, bringing him back around to face you, and point him through your open legs to the target stick again. This time you will circle the target stick around to your right side, clicking as the dog comes around to the right.

Continue to click and treat as your Chihuahua makes the trip around your left leg and then your right leg. When your Chihuahua is traveling around each leg confidently, you can drop out the first click after the dog circles your left leg and just click at the end of the sequence. Cue your Chihuahua to circle to your left side, then immediately send him through to circle your right leg, clicking and treating when he moves into position on your ride side.

Decide what you want your cue to be at this stage. It can be a subtle hand motion—often a modified version of the initial hand target that you used. You may want to fade the hand target to just briefly pointing through your open legs when the dog is sitting in front of you.

You may also use a verbal cue, saying it just before you show the hand signal. After thirty or more repetitions, your Chihuahua will usually move into the behavior when you say the verbal cue, so you can stop giving the hand signal.

Once you have your Chihuahua circling both legs fluently, you can drop out the clicking over a few sessions and replace them with alternate reinforcement at the end of the sequence. Your reinforcement for many of these tricks will be laughing and applause from your amazed audience. Dogs love to show off, and all that attention is often reinforcement enough to repeat that trick again and again, with an occasional food reward.

13 *Five Red Flag Behaviors*

Training isn't always fun and games. Sometimes training is part of a comprehensive modification plan to solve behavior issues ranging from fear to aggression, and many things in between. Behavior modification is effective in changing your Chihuahua's profound behavior difficulties but will require a practiced professional to evaluate your Chihuahua, define his problem, and design the best approach using valid scientific protocols and positive-reinforcement training techniques.

When to Call a Professional

It's not always easy to determine if you have a problem that requires treatment by a professional. After all, many of the behavior problems that you may see are typical or normal dog behaviors that have become unmanageable or just leave you scratching your head. Many perfectly acceptable behaviors for a predatory carnivore are perfectly unacceptable for a household pet, such as aggressively protecting territory or resources, killing small furry animals, or chasing fast-moving objects.

Often, behaviors that leaves you baffled, startled, or worried are the side effects of a stressed, fearful, or confused dog. Many kinds of aggression fall into this category. Addressing the underlying stress and fear resolves these kinds of aggression.

Sometimes, behavior that is manageable or tolerable under certain conditions, like food or object guarding, is no longer manageable in a new environment, say, when you now have children in the home. The dog's behavior hasn't changed, but the level of potential conflict has.

So, how do you know when to call someone to help you? Any of the following red flag behaviors should initiate a call to a behavior professional for investigation. Certainly outright aggression toward people, other dogs, or over toys and food; profound fears, phobias, or anxieties that are not resolving; and any compulsive behavior such as spinning, fly snapping, or habitual chewing should be evaluated. In short, any time a behavior issue is not improvable by some basic skills training, you should seek the advice of an animal behavior professional.

Who Is Qualified to Help You?

Behavior treatment is truly a buyer beware profession. Anyone, yes absolutely anyone, can hang out a shingle and call him- or herself a dog behavior expert, irrespective of training, schooling, credentials, or motivation. The profession is rife with people claiming to be whisperers, pack leaders, master trainers, or doggy psychologists, many with their own secret methods not founded in actual animal behavior science, learning theory, or even basic biology, but based on outlandish interpretations, old wives' tales, and pop psychology.

These types usually have a great back story, like being raised by wolves, being psychically connected to animals, or coming from a long line of expert animal trainers with almost magical powers. Stay away from anyone that cannot succinctly state their professional credentials without relying on an astonishing story of how they miraculously rehabilitated a dog using their special method.

The behavior professionals you should enlist should have some sort of academic or supervised practical background in applied animal behavior, biology, psychology, or education, along with hands-on skills in training dogs. A solid understanding of normal dog behavior is required to evaluate and then modify abnormal dog behavior.

Currently, there are three types of professionals that are equipped to give you support when you are faced with behavior difficulties. Certified Professional Dog Trainers-Knowledge Assessed (CPDT-KA) are dog trainers from a variety of backgrounds that have participated in independent testing and ongoing continuing education. They're required to be well versed on humane training and behavior modification methods, using positive rein-

forcement–based techniques while not using practices that are potentially physically or emotionally harmful to dogs, to maintain their credentials. They will often refer owners to an applied behaviorist or veterinary behaviorist if the problem the Chihuahua has is not a typical presentation, or if they suspect underlying medical, abnormal psychological, or physiological components.

Certified Applied Animal Behaviorists (CAAB) have graduate training in animal behavior, biology, zoology, and learning theory. They are more academically focused than dog trainers, often doing research at universities, and have both graduate training in applied animal behavior and hands-on experience with a wide variety of species. They often work by referral from or in conjunction with a veterinarian on complex behavior issues that have both medical and behavioral components.

Veterinary behaviorists have advanced training in animal behavior after finishing veterinary school. These medical professionals specialize in clinically abnormal animal behavior, diagnosing and treating medical and behavioral problems as well as prescribing medications when indicated to treat those problems. Often, they work in conjunction with CAABs and CPDT-KAs to implement ongoing behavior modification protocols and training.

Any animal behavior professional that you approach should take assessing and solving behavior problems seriously and will require a full behavior evaluation and observation before making an assessment or offering any advice. Stay away from anyone offering quick advice over the

phone, instant fixes based on unscientific information, and false assumptions of your Chihuahua's behavior; they can make your Chihuahua's problem much worse and almost impossible to solve.

Aggression Toward People

One of the more worrisome behaviors your Chihuahua may exhibit is aggression,

especially concerning when it's directed at humans. Many tiny dogs have a reputation of staking out a lap or their owner's arms, or directing their teeth at anyone that approaches them while they are on leash. Although Chihuahuas are small, they can be ferocious, and getting bitten by one is no picnic.

Aggression toward strangers or approaching people can have unintended consequences for a Chihuahua. Though a dog may have initially felt threatened by approaching people and therefore used the tools at his disposal to protect himself or his belongings, he may now carry the label "aggressive."

This label seriously restricts dogs from having a normal lifestyle. They don't get taken out for socialization, or people don't come into the home to visit as often, and this further socially isolates the dog, leading to more aggression because the Chihuahua remains undersocialized and is still afraid of strange people. The only way to break the cycle is to increase your Chihuahua's social life, while changing his perception of people approaching him from "Yikes!" to "Yippee!"

If you notice any sort of aggression directed at other people by your Chihuahua, you should begin a desensitization and counter-conditioning protocol. These techniques help associate the approach or presence of strange people with wonderful things and you may need the help of a professional.

Begin by holding your Chihuahua on your lap, in your arms, or standing next to you on a leash. Feed tiny, tasty tidbits like rotisserie chicken, steak, or cheese, while a training partner, usually someone unknown to your Chihuahua, approaches you from a distance. Continue to feed tidbits as your helper approaches closer and closer over several sessions, always stopping before eliciting an anxious or aggressive response by your Chihuahua. Initially your helper may stop ten or more feet away, but your goal is to have your partner be able to stand right next to you while you feed Fido yummies.

The helper should only come closer, usually a foot at a time, when your Chihuahua is relaxed and concentrating

on the yummies, and should not make eye contact or touch the dog. Have your helper hang out in the new position for a few moments and then walk away, all while Fido is eating tidbits. Stop feeding the tidbits when your helper moves away, since you want the tidbits linked to the presence of the helper.

If at any time the aggression increases or does not begin to decrease quickly while you practice this exercise, you will need to enlist the help of a dog behavior professional. It's possible that there are underlying contributing medical or other factors, or you have more complex behavior issues that need to be evaluated before you continue.

Aggression Toward Other Dogs

A frequent cause of concern among dog owners is their **dog's** reaction to other dogs on the street. They're often startled when their previously mild-mannered Chihuahua is suddenly barky, snarky, and embarrassing when out and about on the leash, often referred to as leash reactivity. So, what's the problem?

Mostly, it's a case of nerves. Nonstop hysterics are a sure sign of insecurity, and your Chihuahua is trying to sound tough. Chihuahuas may be tiny, but they will go onto the offensive if they feel intimidated or threatened by the behavior or presence of a strange dog. Sometimes, something as subtle as the other dog stopping and staring at him gives your Chihuahua that bad vibe feeling, and he has to appear confident, so he barks at the staring dog.

Other times, the **strange** dog is minding his own business, **or maybe** he is having a barkfest of his own, but the owner is pulling him along, so he eventually goes away. Aha, thinks your Chihuahua, the barking worked, that dog went away! The hysterical barking behavior is negatively reinforced because it worked, and away **you** go. **Now e**very time your Chihuahua sees another dog when he's out for a walk, he goes on the offensive, barking like a madman at any dog within fifty feet.

So, once you get over the embarrassment, is it really so bad for your Chihuahua to bark at other dogs? Yes, it's putting him at risk. Whenever your Chihuahua mouths off at another dog, he is challenging that dog. He's saying, "Get lost, or else!" Of course, one of those dogs that

he's challenging will **one day** take him up on the offer, and **it will not be** a fair fight.

Avoid trouble when you're out and about by directing your Chihuahua's behavior, alleviating his anxious behavior around other dogs, and never letting him issue an invitation to a fight he **will not** be able to finish.

One of the easiest ways to manage leash reactivity is with something your Chihuahua already knows: conditioned attention! If your Chihuahua is looking at you, he can't really concentrate on staring at that other dog. You are teaching an incompatible behavior; **this** has the additional effect of lowering your Chihuahua's arousal level, calming him down, so you can then change his perception from "Yikes!" to "Yippee!" Once again, you will practice using desensitization and

counter-conditioning to get this problem under control. If you have not practiced **"Fido, Look!"** and **the** sit-stay in a while, go back and review the attention and sit-stay section in Chapter **10** now, and then continue.

Conditioned attention, or "watch me" is a classic solution to this age-old problem. "Watch me!" is a cue that directs your Chihuahua to pay close attention to you, so you can then direct his behavior by telling him to sit calmly, follow you as you change direction, or simply not engage with other dogs in his presence. Of course, with repetition, your end goal is that your Chihuahua will begin to offer the behavior on his own, decreasing his own arousal level and checking in with you to find out what the team should do.

Start by reviewing **"Fido, Look!"** in a variety of situations. Get it at least

99-percent reliable on one request, in as many locations as you can, before you ever try it with another dog present. After all, if your dog is afraid of something, he can't help but stare at it.

Instead of using other dogs initially, go for a walk in a dog-free zone like an outdoor shopping mall. Use the **"Fido, Look!"** cue every time a person approaches to pass you on the left, next to your Chihuahua. Step aside, ask for **"Look!"** then cue your Chihuahua to sit-stay until the person has passed.

You can click and treat your Chihuahua as the person passes you on the left, and then cue your Chihuahua to move off in heel position to continue your walk. After twenty or so repetitions, you will see that as someone begins to pass you on **the** left, your Chihuahua is looking up at you to see what to do. Capture and jackpot the repetitions that he offers the **look** by himself!

Now you will pick another target to practice with. For the next session, go to a park or school and ask for a **look** and sit-stay every time a pedestrian passes on your left, and every time someone on a bicycle passes you. Click and treat as your target moves past you, and then calmly ask your Chihuahua to move off on your walk. You are building up the distraction level and making it a little harder by making him relax when he sees a faster, more erratic target this time, the bicycle. Again, make sure you jackpot whenever your Chihuahua offers an automatic check-in; it is becoming a habit!

Slowly, begin to move to areas where there may be a few other dogs, at a distance that your Chihuahua **feels safe enough initially to give you the look signal** when asked. Initially, this might be all the way on the other side of the park. Move closer over regular practice sessions, until your Chihuahua can **look at** you in the presence of other passing dogs. If at any time your Chihuahua begins to show anxious, frantic, or aggressive behavior, you have progressed too quickly.

Over many practice sessions, your Chihuahua will learn that passing dogs are an opportunity to offer you the **look** signal, a surefire ticket to high reinforcement. Now he will not only practice a behavior incompatible with aggressing at the other dogs, he will also begin to look forward to the passing dog as a signal that great things are coming his way. Yippee!

If at any time you hit a roadblock in this exercise or are not sure **about** how to continue, you should enlist the help of a professional. Setting up the progressions correctly, keeping the dog moving through the exercises under threshold, and making sure your Chihuahua is not becoming more sensitized to other dogs are critical aspects of success for leash reactivity that you may need help with.

Resource Guarding: Food, Toys, People, and Places

Another of the more common behavioral problems you may run into with your Chihuahua is something called resource guarding. Technically, it's not a problem from your Chihuahua's point of view. Resource guarding is an adaptational

behavior, and it's only natural that any dog would guard things they highly value, like food, chews or toys, their sleeping places, or their favorite people from interlopers trying to snatch them away. Survival of the fittest is in play here, and those with the fastest teeth are the winners in this contest.

The problem is when that competitive drive is directed toward people that have to live with the little piranha. Commonly, it starts out that your Chihuahua growls or shows teeth when in possession of a wonderful gift—a pig's ear, fantastic chew toys, a dinner bowl full of steak, a toy filled with wonderful chicken scraps. Someone unknowingly approaches Fido

he gets growly when he is sitting on the couch and you try to sit down too close? Maybe **he** is fine when Dad is holding him on his lap but snappy when anyone approaches **M**om when she is holding him. **These are all examples of** guarding!

Some dogs will guard many items, all kinds of food, their people**,** and all sleeping spaces. Some dogs are very specific about what triggers a growl, guarding one highly valued item or location.

Sometimes **a** dog has an elaborate aggressive display, giving you clear body language **that tells** you to not touch his stuff**,** by staring, piloerection of the hair from neck to tail, showing a mouth full of teeth and growling. Some dogs, however, especially those previously punished for showing teeth and growling, give a subtle stiffening of the body and then *bam!*, bite you on the hand.

Once you have a list **of** targeted items your Chihuahua guards, post it for all to see. Part of your management protocol is **ensuring** that your Chihuahua never, ever has access to these items, and everyone in the household needs to know what is on the list. If the list is short and **contains** items that you can easily control access to, such as bully sticks or a specific kind of toy, you can stop there. Just don't give the dog these sorts of items. Management can be an effective long-term solution for these sorts of dogs.

If the list is long, you have children in the home, your Chihuahua has actually bitten someone, or the dog guards multiple sorts of resources, such as both food and sleeping places, you need to seek professional help. A behavior consultant will identify at what level your Chihuahua is

while he is enjoying his fabulous find, and he gives a little warning that says "Bug off, and leave me alone. I'm not done with this yet!" This surprising outburst usually stops people dead in their tracks, and then they go away—just the effect Fido was looking for.

Your first line of defense, and to keep everybody safe, is to identify what your Chihuahua is ready to battle over. If regular food is no big deal, but table scraps elicit an aggressive response on approach, take note. If Fido makes faces when you approach him while he has his special beef-basted pig's ear or bully stick, but doesn't mind if you touch his ball or squeaky toys, put it on the list. Perhaps guarding each item, often graded on a numerical scale, and then develop a modification plan to decrease the aggressive response with each item to a level that is safe.

Treatment will desensitize and countercondition your Chihuahua to the approach of people when your dog has the coveted items. The goal is to change his perception from "Yikes, they're gonna take my stuff!" to "I love when people walk by; they bring even better stuff than what I've got!" It will become more rewarding for your Chihuahua to give up what he has than keep it to himself.

At no time should a professional recommend punishment, rough treatment, or threatening the dog for resource guarding during treatment. These techniques would only increase the aggression, adding defensive aggression to the mix and compounding the problem.

Resource guarding can be very responsive to a good behavior modification program and can make your Chihuahua a safer pet. However, success really depends on good detective work with a behavioral history, a thorough understanding of the starting point and end goals, a comprehensive plan, and excellent management while the plan is being carried out. Don't hesitate to get help if your Chihuahua is showing signs of resource guarding.

Fears, Phobias, and Anxiety Disorders

The other commonly presented behavioral disorders include an array of fears, phobias, and anxiety disorders. Dogs can sensitize to, or become fearful of, noise, objects, certain people, threatening movements like hands grabbing them or their collar, other animals, moving vehicles, changes in weather conditions, specific places like the groomer's or veterinarian's office, and anything in the environment that they have had a scary experience with.

Some dogs may have a genetic predisposition to quickly sensitize to fearful stimuli, while you can blow a bomb up under other dogs, and they just wag their tails at you. Poorly socialized dogs are often at risk for developing phobias due to their lack of exposure to novel things during development. They haven't developed those bounce back, adapt to change, coping skills that well socialized dogs have.

Fears and phobias can be long-standing, often starting in puppyhood, or can develop suddenly after exposure to a strong stimulus or traumatic experience. Usually the most effective treatment is based on desensitization, or repeated gradual exposures, combined with counter-conditioning. However, designing a modification program to address those two components can be difficult, and not always possible.

Success is usually dependent on your ability to control exposure to the trigger during treatment, so a program to help a dog fearful of shopping carts, for example, would be more successful than treating a dog fearful of large birds landing in his yard (yes, those are real dog phobias). You can control the shopping cart exposure by starting your modification program on the opposite side of the parking lot, but birds tend to evade your pleading

requests not to land within fifty feet of your front yard during treatment.

Additionally, fears can stack up to create a problem larger than one was by itself. For example, your Chihuahua may have a long history of mild separation distress that doesn't get better, but doesn't get worse, over time. He gets a little worried when you leave, barks for five minutes, then is quiet. Occasionally, he chews up some socks. Additionally, thunderstorms make him a little anxious, but you can usually distract him with a game of fetch and some cuddling on the couch when **a storm** rolls around.

Then, one day when he is home alone there is a terrible thunderstorm. You come home thirty minutes later to a shaking, hyper-salivating, barking, freaked-out dog that has had diarrhea all over the house and has chewed up your living-room drapes. One bad day has triggered an intense thunderstorm phobia, increased his separation anxiety to a new level, including vocalization, destructive behavior, and inappropriate elimination, and created a royal mess that many owners will promptly punish their dog for.

Evaluating and resolving problems such as separation anxiety require a methodical approach. Seek the help of a professional if your Chihuahua has increasing anxiety, or long-standing fear that is not resolving.

Compulsive Behaviors

Sometimes, chronic triggering of anxiety responses can result in compulsive behavior, including spinning in circles, pacing, fly snapping, barking, shadow and light chasing, flank sucking, and excessive licking and chewing.

A dog engaged in compulsive behavior repeatedly performs one or more behaviors over and over, sometimes spending almost all his waking hours engaging in the repetitive behavior. Sadly, the dog may stop eating, become socially withdrawn and physically exhausted, and even physically injure himself.

Compulsive behaviors are often a response to conflict and anxiety about something in the environment, and your Chihuahua may be performing these repetitive behaviors, called stereotypes, because he's anxious and upset. If you punish him, he may become even more upset, and the problem could get much worse.

Compulsive disorders can be difficult to treat and may have a genetic or medical component, as well as a learned compo-

nent. Some breeds have a predisposition to spin, while other breeds may compulsively chase their tail, often catching it and causing damage.

Other breeds may have no underlying genetic predisposition, but the compulsion begins in conjunction with a medical problem. For example, your little dog could have an injury that requires he wear a bandage on his leg. You notice that after you take off the bandage he begins to lick it whenever he is lying in his bed.

Over a few days, it starts to look worse until he has opened the wound and caused damage to the underlying tissue, but he can't seem to stop licking and chewing at the area long enough to let it heal, creating something called a lick granuloma. Even after the wound has healed, he may compulsively lick that area, often causing secondary problems.

Any dog that seems to engage in repetitive, compulsive behavior should be evaluated by a veterinary behaviorist. Treating compulsive disorders can be difficult due to the chemical changes that occur in the brain, and often treatment involves a combination of behavior modification and drug therapy. The possible medical or genetic component, as well as good identification of the stressor that elicits the compulsive behavior, must be considered and treated with a behavior modification program in order to achieve any success.

14 *Spotlight on Chihuahuas*

Chihuahuas are charming little house pets and can learn a few tricks fairly easily, but can they succeed as competitive athletes, in the show ring, or as therapy or even service dogs? Yes! Many Chihuahuas love the limelight, thrive on the teamwork, and excel as performance, therapy, or service dogs. Here are some of the many activities that you and your Chihuahua can participate in.

Agility: Up, Down, and Around

A popular choice of teamwork activity for Chihuahua owners is the exciting sport of agility. Originally styled on equestrian show-jumping competitions, the dog and handler must complete a numbered obstacle course of jumps, tunnels, weave poles, and stationary obstacles.

Dog agility is a growing sport worldwide and requires exceptional training skills to compete at the highest levels. A competitive dog must run the courses off lead and be responsive to the handler's voice and body cues. In competition, the teams are graded on speed and accuracy.

Courses typically have fourteen to eighteen obstacles. The jumps vary in height, from eight to twenty-six inches, based on the size of the dog. Classes are further divided based on the experience of the team competing, with novice, open, and excellent level courses.

In recent years, competitive agility organizations for small dogs have formed to encourage participation for the smallest of our four-legged friends. These venues have challenging courses that are scaled down to be more appropriate for Chihuahuas and other diminutive breeds. Jumps range from four to twelve inches, and are just as challenging, competitive and exciting as what the big dogs face.

Course design can be intricate with a number of difficult obstacles to master for competition. Stationary obstacles with yellow contact zones, called contact obstacles, can be the most difficult to train. The dog must approach the obstacle at full speed but then stop or slow down enough to get one foot in the yellow contact zone. The A-frame, two ramps hinged together, is raised up to six feet above the ground. The dog-walk, three eight-to-twelve-foot planks end to end, is raised up to four feet off the ground. The teeter-totter, or seesaw, is a ten-to-twelve-foot plank that pivots on a fulcrum; the dog must complete this contact obstacle by riding the high end to the ground before moving on.

Tunnels can be either open or closed, and often both appear on the same course. Open tunnels are ten to twenty feet long and approximately two feet in diameter. They are flexible and can be configured in a straight line or curved so that the dog cannot see where the exit opening is.

A collapsed tunnel, or chute, is a cylinder with a tube or fabric attached at the end, extending eight to twelve feet. The chute is closed, and the dog must push through to complete the obstacle.

Jumps can be single-, double-, or triple-bar jumps in an array of combinations on a course. The multibar jumps may have spreads, adjusted for the size of the dog, between them. There are also panel jumps, which are solid in appearance to the dogs. The tire jump resembles a tire suspended in a frame, wrapped in colorful tape to enhance visibility.

The most intimidating obstacle to train, but often the most fun for the dogs to master, is the weave poles. Up to twelve upright PVC poles, also striped to enhance visibility, are placed twenty to twenty-four inches apart. The dogs must enter the weave poles by passing between the first two poles, weaving from right to left and back again, until they pass between the last two poles. If the dog breaks the sequence, he must restart the weave poles at the beginning.

Agility can be challenging training for both dog and handler. The teamwork required, however, is beneficial and rewarding even for novice dogs and their owners, and the basic skills can be learned in a just-for-fun group class or in your backyard.

Obedience and Rally

Competitive obedience is one of the oldest kinds of competitive venues for dogs. First organized in the 1930s as a way to demonstrate the usefulness of companion dogs, modern competitions encourage the high level of training required of a true team.

Obedience competitors are required to show proficiency in a series of basic exercises, including "Sit," "Down," "Stay," "Come," and "Heel," which are evaluated and scored by a judge. Competitions are usually divided into three levels: novice, open, and utility, with the exercises progressively more difficult at each level.

When obedience titles are awarded, an abbreviation is permanently affixed to the dog's registered name. Any dog that achieves over 170 out of a potential 200 points is given a qualifying score for that test and earns a "leg" toward a title. After three legs, the dog achieves the title for that level and moves up to the next level of competition.

The titles awarded may vary depending on which competitive organization the dog is competing under, but may include "CD" (Companion Dog), "CDX" (Companion Dog Excellent), "UD" (Utility Dog), "UDX" (Utility Dog Excellent), and "OTCh" (Obedience Trial Champion). The OTCh is a highly coveted prize among obedience competitors.

Obedience training classes are often held by breed clubs and training schools, with many students going on to compete at the local, regional, and national levels. The training can progress over many years as the team moves up the levels and achieves their titles, but it's rewarding work for both dog and handler.

A related activity growing in popularity that Chihuahua owners can participate in is Rally obedience. In Rally obedience the

competitor proceeds around a course of ten to twenty designated stations with the dog in heel position. Each station has a sign that indicates what exercise the team must complete, and many of the exercises are similar to traditional obedience exercises. Think of it as obedience with a twist!

Currently, there are three levels of Rally competition. At the novice level all exercises are performed on leash. Handlers are encouraged to give the dog encouragement and praise as he continues around the course. At each subsequent level, the exercises become more difficult. At the excellent level the exercises are the most challenging, and the dog is required to work off leash for almost the entire test with verbal praise only.

143

Similar to obedience, Rally competitors earn legs and titles at each level. In this sport, the dogs and handlers begin with a perfect score of 100 points. Points are retracted for exercises that are not completed correctly, with qualifying scores awarded if the team retains at least 70 points.

In the Show Ring

Some Chihuahua owners will enjoy bringing their pint-size show-off into the breed ring. Conformation shows, also referred to as breed shows, are competitions where a qualified judge evaluates how well a dog conforms to an established breed type, as described by a kennel club breed standard. The dogs are not compared to each other, but rather to an ideal representation of the breed.

Though judges have general guidelines on what they are looking for, there is some subjective interpretation. For example, one judge's interpretation of "lively and alert" may differ from that of his colleagues. One judge may appreciate that a coat is "soft and silky," while another judge would think the coat too soft.

Conformation competitors also compete for points toward championship titles. The number of points earned in a win varies depending on what level the dog is at, how many dogs are competing, and whether the show is a major (larger) or minor (smaller show). The exact number of points needed to earn a championship also varies depending on the kennel club offering the title.

Once a dog has successfully won in the breed ring, he may move up to compete against the winners of other breeds in his group. For example, a winning Chihuahua would compete against other breed-ring winners from the Toy group, including Cavalier King Charles spaniels, Havanese, Italian greyhounds, Yorkshire Terriers, Poodles, and Pugs among others. Winners of the group classes then move on to compete against all other groups for the coveted Best In Show award.

Therapy Dogs

While not the typical example, Chihuahuas make a fine therapy dog, especially for the very young, very old, or timid patient. A therapy dog is trained to provide comfort to patients in hospitals, retirement homes, nursing homes, and in schools, to people with learning and emotional difficulties.

While therapy dogs come in all sizes and breeds, not everyone is comfortable when a large, very active, or imposing breed is approaching them. Chihuahuas fit the bill for those patients who are a bit anxious about dog-human contact.

Of course, the most important characteristic of a therapy dog is its temperament. A good therapy dog must be friendly, patient, confident, and gentle. Therapy dogs must enjoy human contact and being petted and handled by strangers. The dog must be comfortable being lifted onto an individual's bed or lap. Chihuahua therapy dogs often excel at the task of performing tricks for their patients.

Several different organizations provide testing and accreditation for therapy dogs.

Some organizations require that a dog pass the equivalent of the American Kennel Club's Canine Good Citizen test and then add further requirements specific to the dog team's needs. Therapy dogs must be well socialized, and testing will require that a dog can tolerate sudden loud noises, walk on various surfaces, ride elevators or escalators, and is not startled by people with canes, wheelchairs, or other assistance devices.

If your Chihuahua has a calm, confident temperament, is very social, and enjoys the company of those in need, therapy dog certification can be a rewarding experience for both of you.

Chihuahuas at Your Service

Service dogs, not to be confused with therapy dogs, are specifically trained to help people who have physical disabilities by doing tasks. In the United States, the Code of Federal Regulations for the Americans with Disabilities Act of 1990 defines a service animal as "any guide dog, signal dog, or other animal individually trained to do work or perform tasks for the benefit of an individual with a disability, including, but not limited to, guiding individuals with impaired vision, alerting individuals with impaired hearing to intruders or sounds, providing minimal protection or rescue work, pulling a wheelchair, or fetching dropped items."

Chihuahuas are adept at some service dogs tasks, including as hearing dogs, as seizure or blood-sugar alert dogs, and as general assistance dogs, retrieving needed items such as medications. Sometimes, service dogs are helpful in minimizing the impact of psychiatric disorders, including panic disorder, post-traumatic stress disorder, and depression.

The most desirable traits found in a service dog include good temperament and trainability. Many Chihuahuas have the qualities to excel in service dog work, depending on the tasks required. Assistance dogs can help a person with a disability gain his independence by assisting him with everyday tasks, and sometimes a Chihuahua is just the right size to be a big help.

Recommended Resources

Books

Don't Shoot the Dog, by Karen Pryor

Reading the Animal Mind: Clicker Training and What It Teaches Us About All Animals, by Karen Pryor

ZOOmility: Keeper Tales of Training with Positive Reinforcement, by Grey Stafford, PhD

Culture Clash, by Jean Donaldson

Train Your Dog Like a Pro (with DVD), by Jean Donaldson

Before & After Getting Your Puppy: The Positive Approach to Raising a Happy, Healthy & Well-Behaved Dog, by Ian Dunbar

APDT's Top Tips from Top Trainers: 1001 Practical Tips and Techniques for Successful Dog Care and Training, by Association of Pet Dog Trainers

Clicking with Your Dog: Step-by-Step in Pictures, by Peggy Tillman

Helpful Online Resources

www.clickersolutions.com

www.clickertraining.com

www.apdt.com

www.dogstardaily.com

www.whole-dog-journal.com

www.drsophiayin.com

www.wadsworth.com/psychology_d/ special_features/sniffy.html

Index